Almost 200 years ago, John Walker had a vision - to blend various Scotch whiskies together to form one superior blend. This newly found art of blending positioned **Johnnie Walker**® Blended Scotch Whisky as the innovator and set the industry pace as an iconic global brand.

Johnnie Walker is a remarkable story of success and leadership founded on elements as simple and natural as the ingredients in the blend. Hard work, honesty, a relentless pursuit of excellence in all aspects of the business, and the willingness to take risks in pursuit of dearly held objectives: these were the values that underpinned the growth of **Johnnie Walker**.

Always wanting to share their vision, the makers of **Johnnie Walker** hope that this book will inspire you to take strides towards making your dreams a reality. The makers of **Johnnie Walker** wish to motivate those with the desire to succeed and help them achieve their vision of personal progress.

- Keep Dreaming
- Keep Trying
- Keep Going
- KEEP WALKING

Best regards,

The **DNA** *of Success*

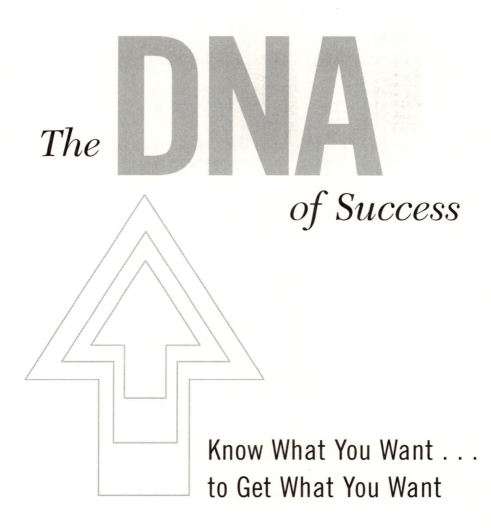

Know What You Want . . .
to Get What You Want

JACK M. ZUFELT

 ReganBooks *An Imprint of* HarperCollins*Publishers*

Grateful acknowledgment is made for permission to reprint from the following:

Excerpts used on pages 16, 21–23, 24–25, 29–31, 34, 49–51, 57, 71, 74, 75–76, 81, 93, 98–99, 152–154, 160–161, 167 were first published in *Executive Excellence* by Ken Shelton and are used with permission.

"Autobiography in Five Short Chapters," copyright © 1993 by Portia Nelson, from *There's a Hole in My Sidewalk*. Beyond Words Publishing, Hillsboro, Oregon. Used by permission. All rights reserved.

This publication is designed to provide accurate and authoritative information in regard to the subject matters covered. It is sold with the understanding that the author and publisher are not engaged in rendering legal, mental health, or other professional service.

Names and identifying characteristics of individuals mentioned in this book have been changed to preserve anonymity.

HarperCollins books may be purchased for educational, business, or sales promotional use. For information please write: Special Markets Department, HarperCollins Publishers Inc., 10 East 53rd Street, New York, NY 10022.

FIRST EDITION

Designed by Kate Nichols

Printed on acid-free paper

Library of Congress Cataloging-in-Publication Data

Zufelt, Jack M.
　　The DNA of success : know what you want . . . to get what you want / Jack M. Zufelt.—
1st ed.
　　　p. cm.
　　ISBN 0-06-000658-7 (alk. paper)
　　　1. Success. 2. Happiness. I. Title.

BF637.S8 Z84 2003
158—dc21

　　　　　　　　　　　　　　　　　　　　　　　　　　　　2002069699

02　　03　　04　　05　　06　　RRD　　10　9　8　7　6　5　4　3　2

To you

and to all that is within you to become

Contents

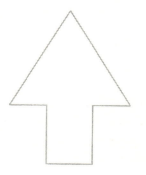

Introduction: Something Is Missing

In quiet, reflective moments, most of us would acknowledge that there is something missing from our lives, something half finished, something envisioned but never realized. This something usually relates to a disconnect between who we are and what we do, between what we want and what we have, or between what we set out to do and what we achieve. We sense that we are underachieving relative to our potential and promise. One constant reminder of this failure is our inability to set and meet goals consistently, to make good on our resolutions, and to keep our promises and commitments to ourselves as well as others.

First, let me ask you three sets of questions:

1. Do you set goals? Do you write them down and read them frequently? Do you achieve many, if not most, of your goals? If you struggle to achieve your goals, then this book is for you.
2. Do you recite affirmations daily? Do you even put them in conspicuous places so you see them all the time? If most

things that you affirm never become a reality, this book is for you.

3. Do you listen to motivational speakers but don't stay motivated when you are alone? If so, this book is for you.

Life presents us with more paths to happiness and fulfillment than ever—yet millions of us still live unfulfilled lives. We are constantly searching for the secret to a life full of happiness, joy, peace, and contentment. We accumulate books, tapes, and knowledge—but not wisdom or results. We have more degrees, but no greater level of success than before. We've learned how to make a living, but not a life. We've added years to life, but not life to years.

Why is this happening when there is a staggering surplus of information, techniques, and methodologies on how to live a rewarding life? There are more "experts" than ever before, yet we still wrestle with the same old problems. In both our personal and our professional lives, we are exposed to a wider diversity of people, ideas, success concepts, and approaches. Still, even with all this abundance, something is missing.

Millions of us search for that *something*, that *secret*, that *special key* that will give us joy, but it stays just out of reach. Sadly, many of us look in the wrong places to find success, happiness, and contentment, and so we become increasingly frustrated. The evidence is everywhere. Consider this:

➡ Nearly half of all marriages fail.
➡ Three of every four working adults are unhappy with their current jobs.
➡ Credit card debt has soared to nearly eight thousand dollars for each cardholder.
➡ Drug and alcohol abuse remain high.
➡ Americans spend more on legalized gambling than on groceries.

Millions of us seem to be saying, "If only I could change jobs, lose weight, earn more money, have a new car, be out of debt, or win the lottery, then everything would be okay." But these things and events aren't the source of happiness. For too long we've put too much faith in wrong ideas about how we can achieve a life that is joyful and meaningful. As a result we are disappointed, disillusioned, and dejected.

Even when we reach the pinnacle of our careers, we invariably ask, "Is that all there is?" We find that the things we worked for—once attained—have little meaning. Then we ask, "What's wrong with me? Why am I not happy?"

What's wrong is that we are pursuing the wrong objectives, going down the wrong paths.

Televisions, bookstores, radio stations, and newsstands are filled with thousands of experts offering the same sound-bite advice on how to attain goals. These gurus all seem to share the same recipes for success: a dash of psychobabble, a sprinkling of gobbledygook, and a heaping portion of positive thinking. The final product resembles a ten-day-old loaf of bread—moldy, stale, and indigestible, with no taste or nutritional benefit. No wonder that after trying the recipe for weeks, months, or even years, we are unhappy and unsatisfied with what we're finding or the results we're getting.

FIVE FLAWED TOOLS FOR SUCCESS

Many teachers of various success methods have told me that they know something is missing because they continually see their students fail, even after doing all they are taught to do.

I have researched all the popular concepts for success and have found that these standard success techniques don't work.

Goal-Setting

Goal-setting is the reigning king of all success techniques. For decades we have been told that if we simply write down our goals and read them daily, somehow we will reach them. My research shows that eight out of ten things a person writes on a goal list will never happen.

Everyone has goals they don't achieve and many they don't even begin to work on!

Amazingly, in the face of overwhelming evidence to the contrary, people continue to believe that if you write down your goals they will happen—and if you don't, they won't. We have all achieved many things that were never committed to a goal list. Writing down a list of goals and expecting each to become reality is an exercise in futility and far too often is a negative, depressing experience. Goal-setting is not the reason people achieve success. Goal-setting is merely an exercise they go through believing, wrongly, that the exercise will make them successful.

How do you feel about yourself when you look at your list of goals six months after writing them down and see that most have gone unmet? Work on some of them may not even have begun, while work on many was started, then stopped. You may have quit in frustration when you realized that the goals you set were harder to achieve than you thought they would be. So how do you feel about yourself when you see that most of your goals never become reality?

No one ever feels good—let alone great—about the fact that they only achieved one or two goals out of ten. When we don't achieve our goals, we tend to redouble our efforts and determine we'll try harder. Perhaps believing our goals were set too high, we lower them, hoping we will now be successful.

Rarely do we consider whether the goal-setting advice was wrong. We always assume that the reason for failure lies within ourselves. After all, if the experts and gurus said this was the way to succeed, who can argue with them? And blindly putting faith and trust in the much-ballyhooed "keys" to success invariably leads us to more wasted time, effort, and money.

Motivational Speakers

Most motivational speakers, entertaining and enlightening though they may be, do not create change in people. After listening to a motivational speaker, most people stay motivated for about two days. Clearly these speakers can motivate and inspire people with wonderful stories, examples, and concepts—but only for a moment in time. Typically they have no lasting impact. Never mind that some of their advice is ridiculous. For example, one speaker says that if you want to stop procrastinating, you should note that assignments are due a couple of days before they are really due. This is like setting your watch ahead ten minutes, hoping to arrive on time. Motivational speakers may entertain and inspire us and make us believe we can do anything, but once we go home and the excitement dies down, the energy dissipates and we are right back where we started.

One young man attended a motivational rally where a speaker espoused ways to make a marriage work. The young man was excited to get this information because he was unhappy in his marriage. He took copious notes. Two weeks later I asked him how those techniques he had learned were working. He replied sheepishly, "I haven't done anything yet. I've been too busy." One month later, I asked him again if the information had helped his marriage. He said, "I haven't applied it yet."

So why do so many of us keep going back to these speakers? Perhaps because we find it exciting to be around our gurus—we become fans, motivational junkies and groupies. Many of us pay huge sums of money for additional courses, even though they give us only a temporary emotional high. We keep hoping that the next session we attend will be the one that finally gives us what we need to be successful.

Self-Help Books, Tapes, and Seminars

Many people have shelves and shelves of self-help books and tapes and supplement these by attending live seminars and workshops. For the most part, these products and events contain great information and valuable insights. However, most self-help books in our libraries become expensive dust collectors. And much of what we hear in seminars is forgotten within days—if not hours—and never applied.

Affirmation, Visualization, and Subliminal Messaging

Many authors and speakers tout affirmations, visualization, and subliminal messaging as important ways to achieve our goals. We are told

> *Your conscious mind gives you the ability to choose, and choice is what controls you, your circumstances, and your destiny.*

that if we repeat positive statements over and over again, they will come to pass simply because we have said them aloud. Proponents of daily affirmations instruct us to say things like, "I have a happy marriage," "I earn eighty-thousand dollars a year," "My mortgage is paid off," and "I am out of debt." If these are not already realities, then what are they? They are lies. The truth may well be that you are overweight, drive a 1989 Chevy Impala, live in a house mortgaged to the hilt, have eight thousand dollars in credit card debt, and are in an unhappy marriage.

Success coaches say that your subconscious cannot distinguish between the truth and a lie, so you might as well tell it a lie if it sounds better, because your subconscious ultimately controls you. I don't know if the subconscious knows the difference between the truth and a lie, but I know the conscious mind knows the difference.

There was a time in my life when I sat with closed eyes and visualized things I wanted for hours at a time. I had visualization down. I could visualize the Mercedes I wanted in great detail. I knew what the dashboard and upholstery looked like, not to mention the exterior color, rims, and tires. I could even smell the newness! I visualized all the things I wanted, and yet I never got them. These mental exercises may feel good, but they don't bring results.

Another popular concept, subliminal messaging, involves listening to ocean waves or the sound of rainfall while subconsciously being bombarded with positive messages, suggestions, and affirmations. Does subliminal messaging work? Maybe, but only if it involves something you really want. Subliminal tapes cannot make you do something you don't want to do.

If your boss wants you to meet a sales quota but you really don't want to do what is required, all the daily affirmations, visualizations, and subliminal messaging in the world won't bring it about.

Enthusiasm, Passion, Positivism, and Discipline Can't Stand Alone

Most motivational experts tell you that you must be enthusiastic, passionate, positive, and disciplined to become successful. You do need all these qualities, and there is no doubt that they are important. But if you don't have the right direction, you are simply treading water.

As you come to understand the DNA of success, you will discard these and other methods that aren't working for you now—and never will—because they are based on false paradigms of success. Am I bucking the system when I disagree with the standard success concepts that have been espoused for decades? Absolutely! I'm saying that there is a better way. Success is not out there in some technique or methodology—it is an inside job. Success comes from within.

That hunger for success in all of us drives a multibillion-dollar industry. But even with all the self-help methods available to us, we are still left hungry for success. We've bought into some strange things, to the tune of $1,145 per consumer a year on personal development products, hoping they will be what we need. But we are looking for success in all the wrong places. Let's stop wasting time, money, and energy, and start seeing the true source of all success.

I encourage you to look inside yourself and discover what you *truly* desire. Find all the wonderful things you've always wanted, and start achieving ultimate success—today!

PART 1

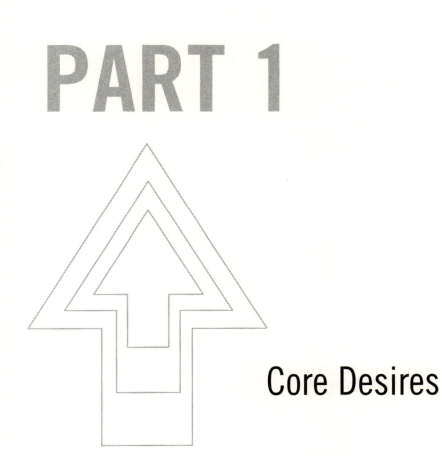

Core Desires

Success Springs from Desire

Success is not the key to happiness. Happiness is the key to success. If you love what you are doing you will be successful. — ALBERT SCHWEITZER

Success is not found somewhere out there—success resides inside, for each of us. You already have what it takes to succeed in life. You were born with all you need. Your birth certificate doesn't come with any guarantees of success, but when you were born you came fully equipped with talents, abilities, desires, and choices. As you grow and progress through every stage of life, you discover that there are things you really want—things you now have your heart set on. As you identify those things and make wise choices, your success is assured.

This book will give you a new paradigm for what it takes to achieve. A paradigm is a way of seeing something—a viewpoint from which you operate. When you embrace a new paradigm, it will cause you to experience quantum leaps of growth and achievement in all areas of your life. With this new understanding, you will move for-

> *"If you want to make small, incremental improvements, work on your behavior. If you want to make quantum leaps in improvement, work on your paradigms."*
> —Stephen R. Covey

ward confidently and quickly, creating the kind of life experiences you want—and deserve. You will leave behind all the wrong paradigms and incorrect concepts you thought were keys to success but that in fact caused you to fail.

WHY WE FAIL

For years I have researched the reasons people succeed and why they fail. In our quest for achievement, we typically make the same mistakes, over and over again.

➡ *We don't know what we truly want.*

    We live in a wonderful time when we can be, do, and have whatever we want. So why do so many of us still struggle to achieve the things we want in life? I believe the primary reason is that most of us, regardless of our age, simply do not know what we really, truly want—we only think we know. It's very easy for us to know what we don't want. It's another matter entirely for us to know what we do want.

➡ *We buy into conventional success methodologies and self-help thinking.*

    We believe that setting goals, affirming goals, visualizing results, listening to motivational speakers, and reading self-help books are the answer. We think that the exercise of writing goals will somehow help bring them about. But the reason we don't achieve most goals is that they are not our *true* desires but merely things that we mistakenly think we want. So we set goals that aren't real to us and start moving down a wrong path. We continue to put our faith, money, and time into success techniques and technologies without realizing that they can't make us successful. Not only do these things not work, but they also create negative feelings.

➡ *We fail to seek or utilize qualified mentors.*

    We listen to the wrong experts—to people whose knowledge, experience, and ability are not aligned with our wants, needs, and desires. Most of these advisers are well intentioned, but they don't know or understand us. They only presume—perhaps based on proximity, intimacy, or psychological assessment—to know what's best for us.

➡ *We expect too much too soon.*

We expect dramatic, short-term results or perfection from ourselves when we most need to be thrilled with any progress. Hot-air promotions that promise "fast," "instant," "free," "easy," and "dramatic" results often inflate our expectations. Almost every product is sold with a guarantee or promise that in ten, thirty, sixty, or ninety days, we will have our desired result. The popularity of cosmetic surgery suggests that many people don't want to wait even thirty days for results, especially if it means submitting to any real discipline.

➡ *We fail to seek feedback and make course corrections.*

Pride so often precedes a fall because we simply won't seek objective feedback, ask for help, or make adjustments, opting instead to keep going until we hit a brick wall or have some other traumatic wake-up call. Then it is either too late to make a change, or very expensive, or both.

➡ *We focus more on what we lack than on the strengths, assets, and resources we possess.*

When we habitually compare ourselves with others who are allegedly the models of how we should look, act, think, or feel, we tend to see all that we are not. We see only our deficits and weaknesses—and if we can't see them, others are often very eager to point them out. We lack faith and confidence in our ability to learn, grow, change, and become whatever it takes to achieve our desires. Our doubts destroy our faith and lead to disillusionment and despair.

➡ *We procrastinate and succumb to the paralysis of analysis.*

When we are intimidated by the enormity of a task—or the reality of a risk—we tend to do nothing but endless and pointless analysis, or at best we make an energetic but futile first attempt.

➡ *We move forward without a plan or strategy and then quit too soon.*

Taking improper action makes it easy to be distracted and hard to maintain focus on what we need to be doing. Having no plan or strategy makes every obstacle appear overwhelming and impassable. We often stop at the first sign of difficulty, whereas had we gone on a little longer and exercised a little more persistence, patience, or perseverance, we would have attained the prize. When we can't see the end of the tunnel, we tend to think that our current condition or circumstance is a permanent state—or that the light we do see is only the light of an oncoming train.

How many times have you tried a product, plan, program, or prescribed remedy for a period of time without experiencing the success promised? When we don't achieve the promised success, we often begin to doubt ourselves. We think we don't have what it takes, that there is something wrong with us. Worse yet, we may see ourselves as failures.

Then what do we do? Far too often we jump back in and reapply ourselves to the same techniques that failed us before—only this time we "try harder." We keep repeating this cycle. We remain stuck in a continuous, self-defeating cycle of effort, then failure, because we embrace a paradigm of success that simply doesn't work.

Incorrect assumptions are the foundation upon which many self-help theories and practices are established. And so we see many people climbing prescribed mountains, only to discover that they don't really want to be on that mountain at all. For them, the climb is always difficult, never fun, and at some point they say, "It's not worth it to me," and quit climbing. Perhaps for them the thought of reaching the top was just a whim, a wish, a fantasy, or a dream. But your desires will only be fulfilled if they are things you really want to do or become.

> "Good thoughts are no better than good dreams, unless they are executed."
> —Ralph Waldo Emerson

Once you discover what it really takes to experience success, happiness, peace of mind, and joy—once you discover the true source of success in all areas of your life—self-motivation becomes automatic. You will let go of all the techniques and methods you have been taught about success.

For example, I stopped setting goals many years ago, and I still achieve everything I want and at a very high level of satisfaction and joy—in all areas of my life. Once you learn the source of all success, you can, too. Everything I have accomplished, I have done without setting any goals.

Goal-setting experts who tell us to shoot for the moon because even if we miss we'll still hit a star ought to be told, "We don't want a star. We want the moon!" What if our Apollo astronauts were these types of goal setters who ended up missing the moon and settling for some star?

Why should we settle for less in our lives when we can learn a better way to have what we most desire? By accepting a star instead of the moon, we are being told to settle for less. Settling for less is simply not acceptable.

THE SOURCE OF ALL SUCCESS

There is a better way to achieve the success you want—a way that is simple and easy to understand because it is basic to your soul; in fact, it is the DNA of all success. It is the way people have achieved success from the beginning of time. It worked before there were self-help experts, it still works today, and it will continue to work in the future. It is the building block upon which all success is built.

Just as DNA is the chemical basis for all heredity, the DNA of success is something we all possess. This DNA of success has been with us the whole time. It is the cause of everything that anyone has ever done or will ever do. Because of it, the pyramids were built, new countries were discovered, men learned to fly and then walk on the moon. It is the cause of millions of other successes less dramatic, such as learning to drive a car, run a marathon, or shoot par golf.

To accomplish what you want in life with any measure of satisfaction, you must identify accurately what it is you really hunger for. If you were lost in a desert, you would soon become hot and thirsty. You would do just about anything to get a drink of cool, clear water. This overpowering thirst is what I call a Core Desire.

Identifying and then wisely, faithfully pursuing your Core Desire is the one success concept that works every time. This is how people have created success for centuries—whether or not they were aware of it at the time. Any time you succeed, you tap into this intrinsic motivation and internal power.

You don't have to write down a list of goals to achieve your aims in life. Basketball star Michael Jordan is just one example of someone who did not set written goals and still achieved greatness. In his article "In Pursuit of Excellence," he writes: "I have the desire to be the best person and player I can become, but I approach everything step by step. It's all mental for me. I never write anything down. I just concentrate on the next step. I envision what kind of person and player I want to become, and I approach it with that end in mind. I know exactly where I want to go, and I focus on getting there. As I reach that level, I gain a little more confidence. Each success leads to the next one."

Michael Jordan first focused on his Core Desire, and then he looked for coaches and mentors who could help him. When he achieved one Core Desire, he moved on, often with the help of mentors. "I'm not afraid to ask anybody (who can teach me something) anything. My attitude is 'Show me, help me, give me direction.'"

All success is a result of four basic concepts:

➡ *First, accurately identify your Core Desires.*

Core Desires are those things you want so badly that you will do, or become, whatever it takes to get them—no matter how hard it is or what the risk. These Core Desires are things that your heart is set on—things you want with all your heart.

➡ *Second, unleash a powerful force that lies within you—the Conquering Force.*

With this force, fueled by passion, you can conquer all obstacles in your way. Without it, you will most likely give in or give up.

➡ *Next, find a teacher, mentor, or coach to help you realize your Core Desires and focus your Conquering Force.*

Without such assistance, especially in the beginning, you may not gain the knowledge, master the skills, or be able to endure hardships and setbacks along the way.

> *"If you do not get what you want, it is a sure sign that you did not seriously want it."*
> —Rudyard Kipling

➡ *Finally, apply the Conquering Force to different areas of your life to make improvements or overcome challenges.*

You will move from one Core Desire to the next in order to learn and experience growth, improvement, progress, and positive change. You will become a more balanced person with the capacity to achieve and sustain success.

If you seriously want something you will get it—it is only a matter of time. When you achieve one Core Desire, you ask, "What's next?" You discover and start pursuing another Core Desire.

These steps make the DNA strands of our success. You can start taking these steps today. You are never too young or too old to begin moving closer to what your heart most desires.

A PERSONAL STORY

Like Michael Jordan, I have achieved everything important in my life and work without any goal-setting. I never wrote down that I would be a professional speaker or author of a book.

My background would suggest that what I have accomplished in life is impossible. I was raised on the Navajo Indian reservation. I was the only Caucasian boy in my high school senior class, and most of my peers didn't like me because of the color of my skin—and because of what the *bilagonas* (white men) did to their ancestors. They held an inherent anger toward me, and I was bullied almost every day.

Each day, school would let out at four in the afternoon. At three-fifty every day, my heart started pounding and I knew what would happen next. As soon as school let out, my classmates chased me, and if I got caught, I got beat up. Recess and gym classes were dangerous times for me—from the time I was eight years old until I was sixteen, I lived in constant fear. At the end of every school day I would ask the teacher if I could leave early and get a head start home. Knowing the situation, the teachers usually let me out early.

One day, when I was ten years old and still in grade school, a boy my age put gum in my hair and slugged me in the mouth. I went home with a fat lip, bleeding and crying. My mother took me to my father, who was working in the trading post less than a block away. My father believed that if I fought back, the bullies would leave me alone. So he put me in the car and drove me to where the boy lived.

When my classmate saw me with my dad, he ran away. My father chased him down and stood him directly in front of me. My dad then tried to make me hit him. "Slug him," my dad said. "Hit him back!" The boy put up his fists in a boxing pose, getting ready to fight.

I refused to hit him. I just stood there with my hands at my sides, crying. I don't know all the reasons why I didn't fight back, but I knew I was simply terrified. My father tried another tactic—fear motivation. He said, "If you don't hit him, I'll give you a whipping." Still I would not hit the boy, and in the end I got that whipping.

Finally my father got angry and shoved me into the car. As he walked around to his side of the car, I heard him mutter, "I can't believe I have a coward for a son!" I can still recall these heart-rending words. He said it with such disgust and disappointment that I grasped how upset he was with me, and I was sure he didn't like me.

I was a coward, and I knew it. My father knew it, too. Everyone knew it. I was teased, taunted, and mercilessly ridiculed. And I thought my father was ashamed of me. For years I lived in fear and shame.

School was never a good experience for me. I did poorly, and my grades were terrible. I was trying to appear okay—to be funny, to fit in some way—so I mouthed off a lot. I got into a lot of trouble with the teachers, several of them making it clear that they didn't like me. My teachers said things like, "You are such a loser," "You'll never amount to much," "How can you be so dumb?" I was sent to the principal's office, and in those days of corporal punishment, I frequently got bent over his desk and paddled with a board.

When I left high school I was convinced that I was dumb and a loser. I understood hardly any math. I just couldn't grasp one concept before they went on to another. I never considered going to college, telling myself, "I'm not about to pay money to go through that torture again." My self-esteem was nonexistent.

When I was nineteen, I took a job as a milkman, and quickly found I hated it. I gave notice shortly thereafter that I was quitting. But my boss at the dairy really liked me and offered me the chance to work at his karate studio as the manager. He offered me a salary and told me that he would teach me how to do the job. And he would teach me all the karate I wanted to learn—for free!

For years I had lived in fear of being beat up and had suffered the shame of being a coward; so when this opportunity presented itself, I didn't have to think about it. I said yes!

I threw my heart and soul into karate. For eight years, that is basically all I did. I had an intense Core Desire to defend myself and regain my self-esteem. No one would hurt me again, and I wasn't going to be a coward anymore! I was driven from within to never again be afraid of any person, to get back at those bullies, and most importantly, to win my father's respect.

My Core Desire was so powerful that I achieved many of the fighting skills of a black belt. Because I was driven from within to learn to fight, I became very good, and I was taught by some of the nation's top fighters.

I loved every minute of it. I was injured many times—I had my nose broken twice, I jammed and sprained nearly every finger on both hands, I broke my left wrist, several toes, badly bruised my shins, and received many fat lips—but I persevered. Did I love the pain? No! But because this was a genuine Core Desire, I never quit. This is the awesome, never-quit attitude that Core Desires bring with them. It's automatic.

I even entered a tournament with a broken wrist. I went to my karate teacher—a seventh degree black belt and world champion—and told him that I wanted to fight but that I was injured. He asked, "How bad do you want to be in the tournament?"

"Very bad," I responded.

"Then do it. You have other weapons. You have two feet and

another fist with which to fight. Go in there and do your best." And so I did, and I lost, but I began to earn the reputation I longed for—that of being one tough guy.

Now that I am older, I know that fighting wasn't my Core Desire. My Core Desire was to not be afraid or be called a coward anymore, to win back my own self-respect as well as the respect of my father. I also found another Core Desire: I wanted to be noticed and looked up to—not just to win fights.

I had no talent, no self-esteem, and no athletic prowess that would suggest I could do what I did or become what I have become, but I did. How can that be? Without understanding it at the time, I had tapped into the energy and passion of a Core Desire and had refused to let my past determine my future.

GRATIFICATION IN ACTION

Most people want instant gratification. The good news is that when you're pursuing genuine Core Desires, in most cases you experience constant gratification. You don't have to wait to have fun or joy when you are on the path leading toward your genuine Core Desire.

Having a life in which everything you do is driven by Core Desires—things you love to do or be—is the most satisfying and fulfilling way to live. When you embark on the journey to identify your Core Desires, you will open up to a new way of living—a life where everything you ever wanted will be available to you or you will be on the path toward it, and loving every minute of it.

You can enjoy that great feeling in every area of your life—going through life working on things you really, truly love or want. There are always the "have-tos" to get to your "want-tos," your Core Desires. If you are dedicated to losing weight or getting in shape, you know you must exercise, but you don't mind this, even if it is hard. Only when your "have-tos" lead to an end result that isn't a Core Desire are you unhappy.

Core Desires inspire action. Throughout history, great leaders have rallied others to their causes, inspired people to accept risks and take action, by tapping into their Core Desires. American revolutionary Patrick Henry revealed his Core Desire for freedom in his famous statement, "give me liberty, or give me death." Most colonists shared that Core Desire. They felt oppressed and wanted to overthrow the oppressor. The closer a leader's vision corresponds with his or her followers' Core Desires, the greater and more powerful the leader becomes.

Leaders have followings because they tap into people's Core Desires. When leaders fail to tap into their constituents' Core Desires, their popularity and influence wane. Smart leaders first learn what their constituents want and then adopt those concepts as their own. Once they know the people's Core Desires, they can promise to help them get what they want.

Most things that are worth achieving require that you put forth great effort. Usually the more worthwhile your desire is, the more effort it will require. You won't put forth all that effort unless you are pursuing a true Core Desire.

There may be many things you have to do to get to your "want-tos." To become a doctor, for example, you have to graduate from college and then from medical school. But if you really want to become a doctor, you don't mind that the path is hard, long, and expensive. Imagine going to college just because it's what your parents want for you. Imagine working at a job that you hate just to get a paycheck that can't support the lifestyle you desire. Imagine becoming a respected professional who earns a lofty income and yet, after years of practice, feels stuck in a rut or caught in a downward spiral, wondering, "If I am doing so good, why do I still feel so bad?" That crisis of meaning often hits after we have experienced some initial success.

Bruce Jenner seemed to have it all. He was the 1976 Olympic decathlon champion who seemed too All-American to be true. He was the man on the Wheaties box and on the cover of *Sports Illustrated*. But in 1980, by his own account, you would never have recognized him.

I was living in the hills outside of Los Angeles, in a one-bedroom bungalow—where the dirty dishes filled the kitchen sink and a dried-out Christmas tree from the holidays four months ago sat in a clump beside the door—serving as the only attempt at interior decoration. I'd lost between fifteen and twenty pounds and years of physical inactivity had left me looking thin. I probably needed a haircut, but living alone with nobody to talk to, I would have been the last to know. I had just celebrated my fortieth birthday, and I desperately needed help. I'd lost all direction in life. I'd lost interest in business, and after two bad marriages, I didn't even want to think about dating. My self-esteem wasn't exactly soaring. In fact, I thought I was so unattractive that I spent thousands of dollars I didn't have on a nose job, only to have the surgeon botch it so badly he had to do it all over again.

Between personal appearances, my life consisted mostly of golf and learning to play a rented piano—I had lots of idle time. I had $200 in the bank, and almost $500,000 in debts. My main source of income was talking about the Games—about how I once was a winner, the man proclaimed the World's Greatest Athlete—while valiantly not letting on how much, and how long, I'd been losing. For somebody who'd won so much professionally, it was amazing how much I was suffering personally. I hoped that nobody could see the defeat and loneliness.

In many ways, I was still the dyslexic kid who lived in fear of being called to get up in front of the class and read. I was right back where I started: stripped of self-esteem, doubting my abilities to make intelligent decisions, and failing in every area of my life.

I had grown accustomed to a life without—without intimacy, without excitement, without adventure, without growth. I was broken as a man. And my medal, the golden symbol of all that I had won, sat in a drawer, now the symbol of how much I'd lost.

I had given up. I had lost my will. But once I hit bottom, I remembered someone from my past: the champion who lives inside each of us, the champion with the capacity to stand before the world in victory. This champion would no longer allow me to live this lifestyle. I saw light at the end of the tunnel and I realized that I could turn my life around and start anew with a clean slate. I was reintroduced to the power that I had experienced, but never understood, so many years before at the Olympic Games. It was a power that would drive me back to the top. It was the power of the champion within, and this power lies deep within each of us. Inside of us, a champion is waiting, ready to rise and radically transform every aspect of our existence. I wanted to become *the best person, husband, father, businessman, and contributor that I could become.*

My life has since blossomed with an amazing ferocity; it was like the angels arrived, the skies parted, and the seas split, allowing me to run through. I have taken my gold medal out of my sock drawer and proudly mounted it upon the wall, allowing it to shine brightly in every area of my life.

For the first time in my life, I know what love means. I thought that it was something unattainable, something that I didn't deserve. Now I know that it is the seed from which all great things grow. I have discovered that our performance in life is a direct reflection of the image we have of ourselves.

Now, I look as good as I feel. I get up every morning eager to tackle my day. From loving my wife to having a meaningful relationship with my kids, to being totally fulfilled in business—life has never been better.

Now I'm not merely in touch with my body but also my heart. And when those two feelings meet, a combustible reaction occurs, allowing me to enter a realm I never thought possible. Somewhere out there, your stadium is waiting, filled with the people you love. They are rooting for you as you struggle, and they'll be cheering as you finally come around the backstretch and finish as a champion.

Jenner's life turned around almost at the instant he identified his Core Desires. Your life can also change for the better when you focus on your Core Desires. You can change your major so you can start enjoying college; you can change your job and start doing something that really appeals to you; you can embark on a new career pursuing what you really want to do and earn just as much or more money in the process. Even if you have to take a pay cut to change fields and pursue your dreams, you will be glad you made the move. You can do whatever you set your heart and mind to do.

Bonnie St. John Deane grew up in hospitals, in leg braces, and on the wrong side of the tracks, but that didn't stop her from believing that an African-American girl, with only one leg, could learn to ski.

As soon as I learned to ski a little, I set my sights on qualifying to compete in the 1984 Disabled Olympics in Innsbruck, Austria. Such an outrageous dream made me stand taller just thinking about it.

My big break came when an elite ski academy in Vermont accepted me as a student. For three months, I searched for grants, scholarships, and sponsors to no avail. When I told the headmaster I couldn't afford the tuition and had failed to find sponsors, he said, "Come anyway." I knew this opportunity would change my life. But then on the first day of the ski school, I broke my leg—my real leg—while playing on a skateboard. As the only kid at the academy with only one leg, I had wanted so badly to show them I could run the obstacle courses, jump rope, and play soccer. Instead, walking on crutches with my artificial leg I could barely get from my room to dinner without tripping. Being so thoroughly inept among a crowd of such superb athletes hurt more than my injuries. At night, I cried in my pillow.

Although the doctor removed my cast after six weeks, my luck didn't improve. A week later, my artificial leg broke in half. Even when you think things can't get any worse, they do. For three weeks my new prosthesis roamed the country, lost in the U.S. Postal Service.

Years later, as I stood on the winner's platform in Innsbruck, Austria, with the silver medal around my neck, I could hear the National Anthem playing, and see the Stars and Stripes fluttering behind me. The desire for that moment had pulled me through all the tough times.

Do you have a powerful desire that captures your heart and picks you up when you fall down? Who or what motivates you? When I am asked that question, I must answer, "I motivate me." For any project you are working on, you can increase your motivation by finding bigger payoffs that have more meaning for you. In all cases, "things" are less important than what those things mean to you personally. List everything you have ever wanted to have in your life: new clothes, vacations, ideal relationships, peak experiences, or career accomplishments. Star the items that really excite you. Find the deeper meaning. Ask yourself, "Why do I want it?" Dig underneath to find the personally compelling reasons. Dig down to find out what you want out of life. Like a child, keep asking yourself "why?" If the final answer is "I should," or "My boss wants me to," scratch it off your list—or change it, expand it, and aim higher. Stop underestimating your odds for success, err on the side of optimism, spend less time around negative people, and learn from people who have done it before you. List your resources and act—don't feel you have to do everything at once. You can get there if you do what you love!

Bonnie's story didn't end on the winner's platform at the Olympics. She has since motivated herself to finish degrees from both Harvard and Oxford, win a Rhodes Scholarship, win awards as an IBM sales representative, and garner high praise as a White House official on the National Economic Council.

Again, it all starts by knowing what you *really want*. Don't get trapped by your present reality—what you have or how effective you are at the moment. People who are immersed in their present realities often think they "know the truth," but they don't.

When you find your Core Desires, your emotion needle will go clear off the chart. Those are the things you'll want to focus on. When you truly want something, you'll amaze yourself at what you will do to get it—nothing will stop you once you uncover your Core Desires and tap into your Conquering Force.

What you will become, or achieve, will be a direct result of the Core Desires you uncover, the mentors you choose to learn from, and the choices you make. Successful people invest in themselves through a continuing quest for knowledge, understanding, wisdom, and truth. When you invest in yourself, be sure you know your Core Desires first. Then you'll see a much greater return on your investment—not only in greater satisfaction but also in improved productivity, enhanced social relationships, and greater earning ability. There's nothing like learning all you can about something you love, your Core Desires. Learning about them will start an important chain reaction that will work in your behalf.

> *"Make no little plans; they have no magic to stir men's blood."*
> —Daniel Burnham

Heart-Set over Mind-Set

*I can teach anybody how to get what they want
out of life. The problem is I can't find anybody
who can tell me what they want.* — MARK TWAIN

When you become aware of the root of achievement, every door you wish to go through will open wide. It truly is the key to success. Whether you use it to open the door or not is your choice, something you have total control over. Whether you choose to open the door or not depends solely on your *heart-set*, not your *mind-set*.

A mind-set is a fixed mental attitude formed by experience, education, and tradition. A mind-set is not the reason you succeed. In fact, it is often the reason you fail. The things you have your mind set on are often either expediencies and emergencies or idle reveries, so your prevailing mind-set lacks the power to sustain effort over time toward the kinds of lifetime achievements that bring real fulfillment. There simply isn't enough passion and emotional power behind a mind-set to clear the pull of habitual "gravity" and launch you into orbit.

Core Desires create emotions that originate from your heart. These are the emotions of intrinsic motivation, the power within. I refer to this as your *heart-set*—or simply what your heart is set on having, being, seeing, feeling, achieving, and experiencing. Your heart-set is a much more accurate guide and source of success than your mind-set—so follow your heart.

Perhaps you have heard people say, "When he sets his heart on something, watch out!" Or "When her heart is set on something, get out of her way." Maybe you have even used this phrase to describe something you really wanted: "I really have my heart set on going to college" or "I have my heart set on having a big wedding." Have you noticed that when you have your heart set on something it usually happens? Why? Because in the pursuit of your heartfelt desires, you exercise real initiative, resourcefulness, creativity, and endurance—you simply find a way to make it happen. You do whatever it takes to get what you want.

Why is great literature so replete with references to the feelings, desires, wisdom, and truth of the heart? Because the heart is the great center of our emotional intelligence and the ultimate arbitrator in the test of truth as we know it. We look to the heart—to our true feelings and our Core Desires—to determine a course of action. We look to the heart when making important decisions. We also look to the heart to assess what's best for us.

The first time I saw my wife, Marci, I was impressed with her beauty. On our first date, we went to a lovely restaurant and enjoyed a delicious five-course meal—and then sat there for another four hours, just talking. We opened up our hearts and discussed things that mattered dearly to us. We both took a great risk by sharing *everything*, including the not-so-good things about ourselves. We probably achieved a greater degree of emotional intimacy in that one evening than most couples do in six months of dating. We fell in love that night.

I had never felt so comfortable with a woman in my life—I felt as if she knew me inside and out. By the time we ended our date, she knew my fears, my failings, and my doubts—including my fear that she might not like what she was learning about me—and she accepted me for the person I was and the person I could be. She also shared similar things about herself.

> *"Few are they who feel with their own hearts."*
> —Albert Einstein

We trusted each other with our hearts, and we liked what we saw. I knew then that I wanted to share my life with her. Five months later, we were married.

I didn't need to make a goal of having Marci for my wife, writing it down and affirming it each day. Instead, I simply followed my heart. Success is all about setting your heart on something you truly desire.

So why are we sometimes so reluctant to follow our hearts? As children, young adults, and maturing adults, we experience heartaches—and they hurt. As a result the idea of heart-set may connote a negative experience, such as the disappointment we feel when something we have our hearts set on doesn't happen. We are then "heart-broken."

> *"I believe that we are like instruments. Whether the instrument is used constructively or poorly depends on us. We have a good mind and a good heart. If we combine these two—the education of the mind and the compassion of the heart—then our contribution will be constructive.... You will have the determination, optimism, patience, courage, and faith to overcome all obstacles."* —Dalai Lama

Marilyn Carlson Nelson, CEO of the Carlson Companies

"You may see me as a woman who has power—the leader of a large company. But the power that matters is the power in my heart. It doesn't matter if you are trying to make a deal that makes a huge difference, or trying to fix a problem within a company. Ultimately, you have to have faith in yourself. You have to have a sense that you will be personally accountable and do everything in your power to influence this world and make a difference. And, you have to know that there's a limit to what you can do and a place where only God can make a difference. If you get that right, you will be successful. Don't let anyone tell you that success has to do with money or power. Success has to do with living on your terms, and ultimately to make a difference. To live your days in such a way that if the time comes where you face some kind of illness, or if something happens that changes your path and shortens your days, that you can say, 'Okay. If today is my last, I'm prepared.'"

*"Only the heart knows
the correct answer. It
takes everything into
account."*

—Deepak Chopra

Carly Fiorina, CEO of Hewlitt-Packard

"At any one moment you often can't see where your path is heading and logic and intellect alone won't lead you to make the right choices, won't in fact take you down the right path. You have to master not only the art of listening to your head, but you must also master listening to your heart. You have all the tools you need up in your head and in your heart. All you have to do is engage your heart and your mind in every decision you make—engage your whole self and the journey will reveal itself with the passage of time. The lesson I learned early in life was to love what you do—or don't do it. Don't make a choice of any kind, whether in career or in life, just because it pleases others or because it ranks high on someone else's scale of achievement, or even because it seems the logical thing to do. Make the choice to do something because it engages *your heart* and *your mind*—all of you. Remember that the freedom to choose is yours. To make the most of that freedom, use your mind and your heart."

Cathy Lee Crosby

"I once lost everything that I'd worked my entire life to achieve—everything I thought mattered—and yet I regained my connection with who I am. It's almost as if the 'wounding' was sacred in its ability to reconnect me with the Divine purpose of my life. We can regain our sense of awe and wonder, our ability to create life from the core of our heart, and reenter the realm of pure possibility. We know that there is a better way to live, but often we keep this thought to ourselves because we are not sure what to do about it. We also know that we have gone outside of ourselves as far as we can possibly go, searching for answers to living a successful, yet meaningful, creative, and connected life. Now we come to the conclusion that there is no other direction to go but inside ourselves.

"I've learned that this circle consists of the Divine energizing each of us, and each one of us, in return, utilizing this dynamic, creative force to glorify, reignite, and reconnect with the pure innocence of living from the core of the heart. The foundation of who I am is now cast in gold, and eternally fired by a direct connection to my heart."

Mihaly Csikszentmihalyi, University of Chicago Professor and Author

"This creativity in the way that you experience life—with originality, openness, and freshness—is creativity that makes life enjoyable, but does not necessarily result in fame or fortune. Everybody can have creativity at the personal level and make his or her life more interesting and more like a process of discovery. When you're creative, you're not always dancing to someone else's tune. You develop your own rhythm of work and rest. For original ideas to come about, you have to let them percolate in a place where you have no way to make them obey your own desires or your own directions. Random combinations are those that are driven by forces we don't know about. Creative people are playful and responsible at the same time. They work not for the result of the work they are doing, or for fame. They work for the sheer joy and exhilaration of doing it. They no longer worry as much about the opinions of others. The drive comes from within, from a sense that 'I have to do this.' It comes from a deep desire to create something beautiful. Each of us can spend our lives doing what we love to do."

MISLEADING MIND-SETS, POWERFUL HEART-SETS

Mind-sets can be accurate from a rational point of view but still be wrong. For example, a management professor at Yale University once responded to a student's proposal of a reliable overnight service that it was a "concept that is interesting and well informed, but in order to earn better than a C the idea must be feasible." Fred Smith went on to found the Federal Express Corporation. In the end, the professor's mind-set was wrong because his idea of what was feasible was limited. What is feasible, functional, possible, or proper to one person may be utter nonsense to a person who is working from the heart.

Your mind-set may be that you must be an extrovert to be success-

> *"If the heart is right, it matters not which way the head lies."*
>
> —Sir Walter Raleigh

ful. Although extroverts can be successful, so can people who do not like the limelight. Some of the most quiet, most laid-back people I have known are extremely successful.

Your mind-set may tell you that good sex is what it takes to have a good and happy marriage. Although sex certainly plays an important role, this is a very limiting mind-set. How you share your hearts is far more important than how you share your bodies.

As you learn to live more from your heart, you will discover the Conquering Force. As you work more from your heart, you will unleash the Conquering Force in your behalf. Let your heart-set, rather than your mind-set, be your constant guide. Let your heart rule your head.

John had very low self-esteem, and he tried to compensate for this by putting others down to build himself up. This behavior was motivated by a Core Desire to feel good about himself at any cost.

John married a wonderful woman, Carol, who grew up with an alcoholic father. Early in their marriage, Carol exhibited some of the characteristics common to adult children of alcoholics. In particular, Carol couldn't tolerate *any* criticism. Even the slightest hint of criticism was devastating to her. For twelve years John, who built himself up by putting others down, and Carol, who was so very sensitive, were at constant odds.

Although John often said he would put an end to his criticism of Carol, the pattern persisted. John made it a goal to stop criticizing his wife and children. He even did daily visualizations and affirmations. Each morning, as John was showering, he would repeat over and over, "I will not criticize my wife, I am a noncritical person, I love my wife and my children, and I will not criticize them." But each morning he would step out of the shower and find something to criticize in no time at all.

> *"For as a man thinketh in his heart, so is he."*
>
> —Proverbs

John then redoubled his efforts, making even more positive affirmations, putting notes all over the place to remind himself, to no avail. John's

Core Desire to feel better about himself was greater than his commitment not to criticize.

In their thirteenth year of marriage, John and Carol stumbled upon some luck. Carol was asked to go to the hospital to help her father through rehabilitation. The time had come for his family to tell him of the pain and sorrow that had resulted from his drinking; it was time for him to accept responsibility.

During all this, John learned to understand how hurt his wife had been by not getting approval from her father. She remembered her father telling her, "I can't believe you're so dumb." Even after she got her bachelor's degree—in his specialty—and excelled in the business world, she felt she had never pleased him. All she ever wanted was his approval, but she never got it.

When John came to understand how hurt Carol had been as a child by the criticism of her father, he was devastated. He felt so much compassion for her he wept. With his new understanding of how criticism made her feel, he made a heartfelt decision *never* to be the cause of that kind of pain or anguish for her. From that day forward, he was a changed man. Nothing else he had tried before had worked. The only thing that ended the years of criticism was when it became a heart-set. As much as he wanted to be positive, his mind-set just didn't have the force to make it happen.

A mentor of mine once told me, "If you think that you aren't getting the things you want in life, you are wrong. You are getting *exactly* what you want."

I took him to task because I could think of many things in my life that I never wanted to happen. At the time I was working at a job that was severely limiting and causing me great stress. The job was just one bad thing.

"How can you say that I am getting exactly what I want in life?" I challenged. I knew I didn't want the job, and yet I stayed there. Once I understood what my mentor was saying, I left the job. I have been working for myself ever since.

Understanding your Core Desires—and how they are the source of true motivation—will help you realize that you may be getting some greater benefit than what you say, or think, you want. For example, you

> *"You will become as small as your controlling desire; as great as your dominant aspiration."*
>
> —James Allen

may remain at a job you dislike because you need to pay your bills.

Charles Garfield, who spent twenty years studying peak performers in every walk of life, wrote:

Inherent talent—an inborn predisposition— is the wiring in one's system that is unique to each individual. One can either identify and develop the specific talents and capacities he or she has, or leave them buried. Peak performers find compelling reasons to cultivate relevant inherent talents. Matching a mission to such gifts greatly enhances the possibilities of peak performance. What often happens is that a vast reservoir of hidden resources becomes available for use.

A baby in action—curious, energetic, reaching out to explore—embodies the inborn urge to grow, achieve, and excel. This motivation need not be taught, but can be untaught or squelched. Peak performers prove that human beings are meaning-seeking organisms. We are not only born in a state of arousal, excitation, and motivation, but we also seek to grow in a particular direction. What determines our direction? Passion and preference—an intense desire to do what we do. High achievers differ in what they call it—passion, preference, deep feeling, or intense desire—but they agree that it determines their direction. They can trace their performance more clearly to a preference than to an aptitude, more to how they feel about what they are doing than what they know.

TURN ON YOUR HEARTLIGHT

Although many people acknowledge that we are born with an incredible, God-given power to do, have, or become whatever we want, no one has explained what it is or how to turn it on. We wonder, "Where is the switch to my hidden energy?"

Your Core Desire is the switch. Having your heart fixed on your Core Desires is how your latent talents, gifts, and abilities are unleashed. Once you have a genuine, clear, and accurately defined Core Desire, you will expend all the necessary effort, for as long as it takes, to overcome any obstacle in your way in order to achieve it.

"Every game, you've got to play from the ground up. Most important, you've got to play with your heart. If you play with a lot of head and a lot of heart, you're never going to come off the field second."

—Vince Lombardi

If you dismiss what you desire most, you also dismiss the very source of your power. Your Core Desires are not wishes, whims, or insincere and artificial goals, nor are they New Year's resolutions that are made with little commitment to fulfilling them. They aren't even wonderful dreams, or things that would be nice to have. Those will not bring results. Your Core Desires are the things in life that really get you excited. When a Core Desire is driving you, things may stand in your way, but nothing will stop you.

OVERCOMING THE ODDS

Colli Butler grew up with alcoholic parents. Her mother went through five marriages. Her father, who had more marriages than her mom did, left when she was a toddler, and she never saw him again. As a teenager, she had such a volatile relationship with her mother that she moved out of the home more than twenty times in just four years. She moved from place to place, often living with friends—always seeking a more stable and happier environment. Her life was hard, to say the least. She overcame seemingly insurmountable odds and this emotionally unstable background to become a highly successful woman in network marketing. And she has maintained a very happy and healthy marriage.

By the time she was ten, she had seen women whose lives were full of suffering, sometimes brought upon themselves by making wrong choices. Colli learned from those negative examples and vowed never to make those mistakes herself. She got involved in building the spiritual area of her life, which has continued to make a positive impact on all areas of her life. She went after her success with all her heart.

OH, WHAT A FEELING!

We all have the innate ability to achieve what we most desire, no matter what barriers exist. When my son was twenty-two years old, he wanted to buy a truck so he could start a lawn care business. His Core Desire was to be more independent and self-sufficient, but he needed to buy a truck. His former boss had a great truck. Having seen that truck at work, he knew that he needed one just like it.

My son and I went to almost every dealership in the Denver area, to no avail. Although my son had excellent credit, he had no credit history. No dealership would finance him without a co-signer. When he asked me to co-sign, I turned him down. I told him I didn't believe in making things so easy for children that they were robbed of the chance to stretch and succeed on their own. I offered to loan him money for a down payment if he needed it to secure financing.

For two weeks every car door was slammed in his face, so to speak. He was naturally discouraged, but he refused to give up. Finally he decided to call his old boss to ask if he knew of any way he could get a truck like his. His boss said that he had recently purchased a new truck and that the old one was just sitting in his driveway. He then offered to sell it to my son—and even to carry a contract on it! Within hours, my son closed the deal and ended up getting the very truck that had inspired him in the first place. Such is the strength of a heart-set. When your heart is set on something, you don't give up. You fight, dig, and scratch until you get it. Sometimes these things require blood, sweat, and tears. But when it is your heart-set, you will always find a way to make it happen.

KARATE FOR THE HEAD OR HEART?

> "If you care enough for a result, you will most certainly get it."
> —Robert Collier

Many years ago, when I was teaching karate, I could usually tell how well my students would perform from their motivation to learn in the first place. Often it was just a passing fancy, an ego trip, or a belt. But for others it was a burning desire.

Once, a university professor approached me and told me he wanted to become a black belt in karate. In fact, he confided, it had been his goal for over fifteen years. Now, for the first time, he inquired what it would take to make his goal a reality. I told him that to achieve this distinguished rank in karate, he would need to dedicate at least one hour a day for four years. He was visibly disappointed. After a moment, he said, "I had no idea it would take that kind of effort." He walked away and never again pursued karate. He had committed a wish to paper and somehow hoped it would magically happen, but he hadn't even bothered to learn what it takes, let alone start on the path. When he discovered the amount of work, commitment, and time required to achieve a black belt, he lost interest and gave up.

One week later, Mark Porath, a strapping fourteen-year-old, approached me and asked the same question. When I told him it would take him two hours a day and five years of his life, he responded, "Is that all? When can I start?"

Mark's heartfelt desire to earn a black belt was a Core Desire for him, and he went after it wholeheartedly. He was willing to do whatever it took to make it happen.

Five years later, Mark was one of the best black belts I had ever seen. He went on to become the state champion, winning nearly every tournament he entered. Mark never wrote down that he wanted to be a black belt—he just wanted it with all his heart and went after it, not letting any obstacles stand in his way.

Mark's Core Desire originated from a serious physical disability. When he was born, his feet did not face forward but pointed outward. Until he was nine years old, the way he walked earned him the nickname "Penguin." Because of his problem, he couldn't run and play like the other kids, he could only watch.

When he was nine years old, Mark underwent an amazing operation. Doctors surgically turned each of his legs and feet forward. He was in a body cast from his chest to his ankles for nine months. When they removed the cast, his muscles had atrophied and he had to learn to walk all over again. This experience left Mark with little coordination. Unless he was leaning against a wall, he couldn't lift either of his legs without immediately losing his balance.

Mark came to me wanting to learn karate, but without something to lean on, he would begin to fall when he began a simple kick. Before he could recover from a poorly executed kick, he would fall down. Suffering from a deep feeling of physical inadequacy and a lack of self-esteem, he was angry at the world.

But his desire to master karate came from deep within his heart. His lack of self-esteem drove him to excel. He wanted to be the best at karate—to prove to the world that he could be really good at something.

This is what a heart-set looks and feels like. How else could Mark have invested so much time and effort, in spite of his physical challenge, and attain such a high pinnacle in karate?

OVERCOMING BARRIERS AND OBSTACLES

There will always be barriers and obstacles between where you are right now and where you want to be. If your desire is fairly strong, you will definitely get started on it. You will probably spend a lot of money and time on it, too. You may even get most of the way there. However, the day you encounter a barrier or obstacle that is bigger than your desire, you will be stopped. That's the bad news. The good news is that there are no barriers or obstacles that can stop you when you are pursuing a Core Desire. The obstacles you encounter may be intimidating, they may slow you down, they may be difficult, they may hurt like crazy—but they won't stop you if you focus on your Core Desires.

When you are less than wholehearted, you are easily derailed.

When your whole heart is committed, failure is not an option. Halfhearted athletes or teams will never become champions. A halfhearted relationship just doesn't cut it. A halfhearted salesperson is destined to a life of mediocrity and financial struggles. Halfhearted will only get you halfway there. Anything less than wholehearted is destined to mediocrity or failure.

> "Obstacles cannot crush me. Every obstacle yields to stern resolve."
> —Leonardo da Vinci

Every obstacle yields to stern resolve, and resolve comes from Core Desires. The ability to make obstacles yield comes from your Core Desires and Conquering Force.

In 1989 Melissa Poe saw a television show about what the world might look like in twenty years if our current levels of pollution continued. Melissa became very upset, and she decided to write President Bush, asking him to put up signs saying, "Stop pollution. It's killing the world."

After not getting a reply from the president, she thought perhaps her letter had been lost in the mail and decided to put up her own signs. She called an advertising agency in Nashville, Tennessee, and asked them if they would put her letter to the president on a billboard. When they asked her what organization she was with, she created Kids FACE—Kids For A Clean Environment. After they caught the vision of what Melissa was doing, they agreed to help. She then asked them if they would put one up in Washington, D.C., where the president lives.

The agency told her they didn't have any billboards in Washington, D.C., but they gave her the name of a company that did. Melissa called them all and got them to agree to put up their own billboards. She kept getting more names of billboard companies and began calling them. Within a few months, over 250 billboards across the United States displayed her letter to the president.

Melissa also tried to enlist the help of environmental clubs, like the Sierra Club and Greenpeace, but they each told her she would have to wait until she was older. At the time, Melissa was just nine years old.

> "Where your treasure is, there will your heart be also."
> —Matthew 6:21

When Melissa started Kids FACE, there

were only six members. But by the time she was sixteen, it had grown to over two hundred thousand members worldwide, and her newsletter went out to over two million people.

Both Mark and Melissa had their hearts set on something, and their minds never told them they couldn't succeed. Following their examples, we should all listen to our hearts. If we listen first to our minds, we will probably be led astray by the facts.

Thinking you want something that at the core of your heart you really don't want creates a huge problem. People write down goals as if they know what they want, but they really don't. Most goals never come to pass because they aren't genuine. They don't come from the heart. Desires that come from the heart come to fruition. They become reality because you really want them.

Success, then, does not come from wishes, whims, impulses, goal-setting, daily affirmations, visualizations, intimidation, or pressure. Nor is it merely something that "would be nice to have." The DNA of all success is the combination of Core Desires and the Conquering Force.

> *"Your own resolution to succeed is more important than any other thing."*
> —Abraham Lincoln

Identifying Your Core Desires

There is only one success—to be able to spend your life in your own way.
—CHRISTOPHER MORLEY

Core Desires are those things you have your heart set on—what you want to be, have, or do most. One might think that identifying these Core Desires would be easy, but people often tell me, "I don't know what I want, please help me." This dilemma affects people of all age groups and crosses all political, social, and economic lines. People tell me that they don't know what they want to be, have, or do when they "grow up." They are still searching.

NO SENSE OF OBLIGATION

Core Desires aren't objectives imposed on you by others. They aren't "shoulds" or "ought-tos." Core Desires are those things you want with all your heart. They are deep, intense, and powerful longings. They are persistent, ever-demanding, heartfelt hungers or yearnings that pierce you to the very core. One easy way to identify them is that they are always tied to a strong emotion in your heart—which is the reason any-

"The hand will not reach for what the heart does not long for."

—Old Welsh proverb

thing in your life gets done at a high level of success, satisfaction, and fun. The Conquering Force is the only force strong enough to sustain the persistent effort and focus necessary to realize your Core Desires.

However, people often do things because they feel they have to, ought to, or should, not because they truly want to. It could be because they feel a duty or obligation or because they fear punishment, ostracism, or disapproval.

Your life is too precious, and your sojourn here on earth too short, to waste your time and effort on things that are not rewarding and fulfilling. Yes, at times you must "do your duty" with family, friends, employers, and country—but duty is pleasure when it aligns with desire.

We will always encounter some "have-tos" on our way to our "want-tos"—our Core Desires. That's a fact. Some duties may be unpleasant, difficult, expensive, or even painful. But you won't mind doing them if you are getting where you want to go.

If your heart is set on getting a college degree, you will have to take some courses you don't like. If you want to get into shape, you will have to exercise. If you want to lose weight, you will have to change your diet. If you want to own your own business, you will have to take certain risks. However, you won't mind the "have-tos" while pursuing your Core Desires because the rewards far exceed the price to be paid.

When the "have-tos" aren't getting you to your Core Desires, your life is less fulfilling. It may even be miserable. Only when you are pursuing your Core Desires—those things that inspire you and bring you joy—will you unleash the powerful Conquering Force within you. You will experience profound joy, peace, balance, serenity, and happiness. As you pursue the desires of your heart, you will be happier.

What makes work *work*? When you don't like it. When you love doing something, even if it is physically or emotionally demanding, you don't mind the effort required; in fact, you may call it fun.

To experience a life full of enjoyable activities, day in and day out, you must know what you really desire. If you think you want something, but deep down at the core that's not really what you want, you will never attain it.

WHAT DOES YOUR HEART DESIRE?

Do you know what you desire most in your heart?

Do you have a sense of what it will take to realize those desires?

Are you willing to pay the price?

For example, suppose you want to become a certified public accountant. You know that you need to complete a course of study as well as pass certain tests to realize this desire. Now you need to ask, "Am I smart enough to learn what I need to know? Do I believe that the knowledge I need already exists somewhere in a class, a course, a book, a seminar, a mentor, or on the Internet?" If you answer these questions with a confident yes, you clearly have the ability to achieve your desire to become a CPA. Next, you will need to put your ability to learn anything together with the information that already exists. The catalyst for all this comes from your Core Desires. If you have had a goal for months or years and haven't learned what it takes to make it happen—let alone started working toward it—it is not a Core Desire.

Drilling down to your Core Desires and exposing them to the light of day can be, at least until you get the hang of it, a little difficult and emotionally frustrating because you are not used to dealing with your feelings at the core level. So I have designed a measurement device to help you identify your Core Desires. This simple assessment tool serves as a guide to finding and knowing your heart's desires—it causes you to reflect on everything you would like to have, do, experience, become, or achieve in many areas of your life. To help you assess the relative intensity of those desires, I have also designed the Core Desire Scale.

A GAME OF QUESTIONS

Identifying your Core Desires can be as easy as honestly answering these two Core Desire Search Questions:

1. *What would I like to have that I don't have now?*

You might ask this question to help you uncover your Core

Desires in different areas of your life, such as family relationships, finances, self-image, social relationships, mental self, and spiritual self. This list isn't all-inclusive, but it illustrates areas in which identifying your Core Desires could prove beneficial.

With this central question in mind, try answering these questions to learn what you truly desire most:

→ What would I love to do if I had no obligations? If only I had more time?

→ What makes me very happy? What makes me laugh?

→ What tugs at my heart or stirs my emotions? What am I pining away for?

→ What would I love to do to help others?

→ What characteristics would I like to have or strengthen?

→ What do I want with or from my spouse and children?

→ What do I want with or from others?

→ What do my best friend and I do for fun?

→ What did I used to do that I just can't do now?

→ If I didn't have to worry about money, what would I do?

Each of these questions will elicit strong responses—but not all of them are Core Desires. Ask this next question about each desire you have just identified to narrow the field:

2. *If I had that, was that, or could do that, what would it give me and how would it make me feel?*

Asking this second question helps you get past superficial wants and wishes and helps you see what difference this desire, once fulfilled, might make in your life. But your search is not over; you must now measure the strength of these desires.

THE CORE DESIRE SCALE

You must be very sensitive to the intensity of your emotional responses to each of the Search Questions. This sensitivity will help you accurately measure the intensity of your desires. Intensity is everything as it relates to the achievement of your Core Desires.

What a difference a degree or two of intensity can make in the results you achieve for your efforts! If you want to cook some vegetables or power a steam locomotive, you must heat the water to 212°F to make the water boil—211°F is very close, but it won't do. Only when the temperature reaches 212°F will the water begin to boil, bringing the results you want. If the temperature is between 95°F and 106°F, then the water is only lukewarm.

The seismograph, or Richter scale, measures the magnitude of an earthquake. The scale measures magnitudes of 0 to 10. Why is the difference between earthquakes measuring 5 and 7 on the Richter scale so dramatic? Because each number on the scale represents an earthquake ten times stronger than the number just beneath it. An earthquake registering a 7 on the Richter scale is ten times more powerful and ten times more destructive than one registering a 6. Imagine the power of the most powerful earthquake ever recorded— an 8.9 on the scale.

Just as the Richter scale measures an earthquake's intensity, so must you assess the intensity of your desires, feelings, and emotions by using the Core Desire Scale, which has a range from 1 to 100:

1 to 20: whims, passing fancies, wishes, gratifications, momentary pleasures, and dislikes

20 to 40: shoulds, oughts, duties, obligations, assignments, and extrinsic motivation

40 to 60: moderate-intensity desires, wants, interests, and needs

60 to 80: recurring desires, growing intensity, strong mind-sets, and a sense of duty

80 to 99: Steady desire; relevant, important initiatives; strong interest and motivation.

100: high intensity, relevancy, immediacy, heartfelt, passionate, and dead earnest. These are Core Desires.

The things you hate and would never do in a million years are 1s on the Core Desire Scale. Things that you are sort of interested in and may like to have—anything about which you feel halfhearted or not totally committed—are somewhere between 40 and 80 on the scale. These are like 5s on the Richter scale. Core Desires are always 100s.

The 100s on the Core Desire Scale are like the 10s on the Richter scale—far more powerful than a want or a wish. A 100 is infinitely more powerful than a 90 on the scale. When you pursue desires that fall below 90 and encounter the inevitable problems and barriers, you will find that you don't have the ability, or the drive, to move past them. You will get discouraged, give up, and hang negative labels on yourself. A 90 may get you 90 percent of the way there, but any desire that is not 100 will not have the ability to unleash your full internal power—the Conquering Force.

These desires that measure 100 are *the* source of your undying enthusiasm and discipline. They are the only desires that will provide you with the persistence, and ability, to overcome any and all obstacles. The intensity of these Core Desires will breathe life into your project, your family, your plan, your religion, your business, and your life.

Once you gain the skill of recognizing your 100s on the Core Desire Scale, you won't have to go through the search questions and scale exercise again, but sometimes you will have to repeat the search questions several times to get to your Core Desires. It's like drilling through layers of sediment to reach bedrock. You may hit bedrock right away, or it may take several tries. How quickly and accurately you identify your Core Desires depends solely on how quickly you get out of your head and into your heart.

THREE EXAMPLES

1. *In the financial area of your life, what would you like to have that you don't have now?*

    If you answer, "To be financially independent," this may rate an 80 on the scale, but it is not your Core Desire. Now ask yourself the Search Question: "If I were financially independent, what would that give me that I don't have now?" You may answer, "It would give me the freedom to do what I please."

    Using the Search Question again, ask yourself, "If I were free to do as I please, what would that freedom look like? What would that give me that I don't have now?" This is where people get stuck. Often they have a hard time clearly defining their answer, so they repeat themselves.

If you find yourself getting stuck, just ask the question in a different way: "If I were financially free, what would that give me that I want but don't have? What *feelings* would that give me?"

You may say, "Oh, I know! I could spend more time with my family!" Or "I could quit working at a job I hate." These emotional responses are your *Core Desires*. These are the 100s, and you should only spend your time and energy pursuing desires that hit the 100 mark on your Core Desire Scale.

If your answer were "If I were financially independent today, I'd be free from the stress and worry of not paying the bills," you'd not be far from your true Core Desire. But what words jumped out at you as you read that last answer? Were they *paying the bills* or *free from the stress and worry*?

If you chose the latter, you would be right on. However, there are many ways to reduce stress and spend more time with the family, even without being financially independent. Being financially independent would be nice, but what you really want is to be free from the worry, stress, or guilt of not being with your family as much as you would like. Knowing that stress and worry are the real issues could give you many more options for achieving those Core Desires.

It doesn't take being financially independent to be free of guilt or worry. You may need more money, but just how much more money would it take? You'd be surprised by what saving two hundred dollars a week—or month—would do. It might take some aggressive budgeting or reducing your car payments by selling your second car. Just changing your attitude can rid you of heaps of worry and stress.

2. *In your social life, what would you like to have that you're not getting now?*

You may answer, "I just love helping others, and I'd love to do that more." Again, this may be a 90 on your scale, but it is not your Core Desire. Ask yourself, "If I were able to help others more, what would that give me or make me feel that I am not getting or feeling now?" You may answer, "It makes me feel happy." Try asking the question again, phrasing it differently: "Why do I love helping others? What other feelings do I have when I am helping others?"

Keep digging, and keep asking the Search Question. You may find your answer with "I love helping others and putting smiles on their faces" or "helping others makes me feel good." Maybe even "I love the positive feedback I receive." All of these may be high on your scale, maybe even 90s, but they are not your Core Desire.

Ask yourself the Search Question this way: "Why do I love the positive feedback?" Or "Why does it make me feel good?" When you answer, "It makes me feel valuable, important, or appreciated," these are the real Core Desires.

Often people who don't feel valuable or appreciated seek ways to meet those desires by helping others. No wonder they want to do it more: the real Core Desire is to feel needed by others. This is a definite 100 on the Core Desire Scale.

3. *In the area of self-esteem and self-image, what would you like to have in your life that you don't have now?*

You may say, "I'd like to be more confident around people." Though this may be true, it is not a Core Desire.

Ask the Search Question, "If I were more confident around people, what would that bring me that I am not currently getting in my life?" You answer, "I would be willing to speak up more and have my opinions heard." By continuing to ask the Search Question, you are getting closer to identifying your true Core Desire.

Keep asking yourself the question: "If I were willing to speak up and have my opinions heard, what would that give me that I don't have now?" You may say, "I wouldn't feel like I'd let others or myself down by not speaking my mind." You're getting higher on the scale, but you're not quite at 100.

"How do I feel when my opinions are not heard or when I am put down?" You may answer, "I feel bad and unimportant—like my opinions don't matter." These are strong emotions and evidence that you are on the right track.

When you ask the question "To whom do I want my opinions to matter most?" you may answer, "My spouse. Having my thoughts and feelings heard and validated by my spouse is very important to me." You have found your 100, the thing that matters most.

This desire has a lot to do with having a safe, uplifting, and intimate relationship and little to do with self-confidence. If your focus is on confidence, you have set the wrong goal. All your pursuits of confidence probably won't get you the validation you want from your partner.

This validation is gained much faster once you realize that confidence is not your Core Desire, but the need to have a healthy, happy, personally validating, I-feel-important relationship with your spouse. Many people are very confident in their work but feel deprived in their marriage or other personal relationships.

You may have to ask the question "If I had that, how would it make me feel?" several times or several ways until you've drilled down to the core and discovered your Core Desire. As you learn to become aware of your true feelings on any subject or issue, this exercise will become second nature. You are then in a position to live an authentic life.

Warren Bennis, distinguished professor of business administration, University of Southern California and author of *On Becoming a Leader*

"I believe in self-invention as an exercise of the imagination. That's basically how we get to know ourselves. People who can't invent and reinvent themselves must be content with borrowed postures and secondhand ideas, fitting in instead of standing out. Inventing oneself is the opposite of accepting the roles we were brought up to play. To be authentic is literally to be your own author, to discover your native energies and desires, and then to find your own way of acting on them. When you've done that, you are not existing simply to live up to an image posited by the culture, family tradition, or some other authority. When you write your own life, you play the game that is natural for you to play. You keep covenant with your own promise."

Bennis cites studies that underscore the benefits of self-invention.

First, studies show that middle-aged men tend to change careers after suffering heart attacks. Faced with their own mortality, these men realize that what they've been doing and what they've invested their lives in are not accurate reflections of their real needs and desires.

Another study indicates that what determines satisfaction in men past middle age is the degree to which they acted upon their youthful dreams. It's not whether they achieve their dreams but the honest pursuit of them that counts. The spiritual dimension in creative effort comes from that honest pursuit.

Women, too, are happier when they "invent" themselves rather than simply accepting without question the roles they have been brought up to play. Historically, remaining single has been a way for most women to invent themselves. Changing times have meant changes in relationships, too.

Dave Thomas, founder of Wendy's, Old-Fashioned Hamburger Restaurants

"Excellence in any one little thing is hard enough. Know what motivates you and prove to yourself that this motivation is honest and worthwhile. If you do it for praise, you are likely to shortchange yourself in the end. Don't allow people's opinions about you to sidetrack you. Just be yourself, and you'll be much happier. Inside yourself, you have to have a clear understanding of where you want to go and confidence in your ability to get there."

Oprah Winfrey

"Be who you really are. Life is just about having everyday experiences, and these experiences teach you, moment by moment, who you really are. Every experience in life teaches you more fully how to be who you really are. For a long time, I wanted to be somebody else. Growing up I didn't have a lot of role models. I was born in 1954. The only Black person on TV then was Buckwheat. I was ten years old before I saw Diana Ross on the *Ed Sullivan Show* with the Supremes, and I said, "I want to be like her." It took me a long time to realize I was never going to have Diana Ross's thighs, no matter how many diets I went on. I came to realize that I could only be me—not Diana Ross or Barbara Walters. Through a series of mistakes, I learned I could be a much better Oprah than I could be a Barbara. I allowed Barbara to be a mentor for me, as she always has been, and I decided then to try to pursue the idea of being myself. I had to recognize that instinct or inner voice that told me, 'You need to find a way to answer to your own truth.' "

Christopher Reeve

"Some people really don't know what they want to be. When they are asked, 'What are you going to do with your life?' they have the honesty to answer, 'I really don't know.' Such honesty can lead to very rewarding and profound discoveries about yourself."

THREE CASE STUDIES

Uncovering your Core Desires and unleashing your Conquering Force will cause you to live a fuller, happier, and more successful life. As you learn to identify, and pursue, your Core Desires, you may find yourself in any of these three situations.

Right on the Money

Once, a vice president of a large insurance company came to me and asked for my help. Although he was earning more than enough money, he wasn't happy in his job. He had been at it for twenty-two years and had just grown tired of it. He wanted something else. When I asked him what else he'd like to do, he replied, without emotion, "I've been looking at real estate and investments because I know people who have succeeded in those areas."

When he admitted that he had chosen those two professions because he had seen others do well in them, I told him, "You might want to consider another option. There's no emotion at all in your voice. Your head is talking, not your heart, and these options don't reflect your Core Desire."

"Well, then," he said, "I guess I just don't know what I really want to do."

"What gets you all jazzed up and excited?"

Suddenly his face lit up as he said, "My heart starts to pound when I think about doing this one thing because it's so exciting to me." Before telling me what this one thing was, he added, "But I don't see how I can continue to make a good living by doing it."

"Scratch that last sentence. Just tell me what it is," I said.

"I love to speak in front of people. I've been to Toastmasters and taken Dale Carnegie courses. I'd really love to be a public speaker and help people in their lives. That's what I'd really love to do, but I don't see how I could make it work and stay financially secure."

His mind tried to sabotage his Core Desire, but we quickly discovered what his heart wanted most. I asked, "Do you know anybody who's making a living as a speaker?"

"No," he said.

"I do, and I will be glad to share with you how to do it. Believe me, it has been done, and you can do it, too."

He then asked me to teach him.

Close but No Core Desire

A young woman was trying to find her Core Desire when it came to earning a living. At the time, she was doing a job she enjoyed but did not find soul satisfying.

"What would you really love to do? Is there something that would bring you greater happiness?" I asked her.

She said she didn't know but mentioned how much she enjoyed her volunteer work with abused children. "If I could do that for a living, it would be wonderful. I would really like to spend my life helping those children and maybe I could have my own child center."

It was easy to tell from the animation in her voice and the radiant expression on her face that this was a Core Desire. I told her that this is what she should go after.

"But I'm too young, I don't have a license, and I don't have the money," she said.

Although these were real barriers, I told her, "It doesn't matter what problems you encounter, because there are always solutions. You will find a way when you're pursuing your true Core Desire."

Passing Fancy

After one of my seminars, a young man came up and asked me if he could follow me around. He told me that he wanted to "become just like me." He wanted me to be his mentor.

Although flattered, I suspected that this momentary glow would not last. I agreed to help him, but first I gave him some homework. His assignment was to go home and familiarize himself with my program. After he completed this, he was to call me and arrange to spend the time he wanted.

I never heard from him again. This young man's request was a wish—a mere whim. Once he discovered the work it would take, he forgot about it and stopped working toward it because it was not a 100 on the scale.

EMOTIONAL VALIDATION

How will you know when you've hit pay dirt? You will know when you arrive at the core because you will invariably have some kind of emotional reaction. Our Core Desires always center around how we want to *feel* about ourselves—as a result of being a certain kind of person, having a particular item, or accomplishing a particular thing.

When you identify a Core Desire, you may feel great joy. You may even start to cry, because the long hidden need or want has gone unfulfilled for so many years. You may get sweaty hands, or your heart may pound with excitement. Sometimes discovering a Core Desire is accompanied by just a calm, peaceful sigh of understanding or a simple, clear, doubt-free, quiet nodding of the head.

Ask someone who knows you well to help you evaluate your emotional responses. Their observations of your emotional reactions can be quite accurate. No matter how you react to discovering your Core

Desires, you'll know it when it happens. Fathoming a Core Desire takes introspection, work, empathy, and insight.

Identifying your genuine heartfelt Core Desires requires that you really get to know yourself—at levels you might not have gone to before. What is way down there can be a real eye-opener. It may be humbling, embarrassing, or may open old wounds. In each case, it is valuable because it is the truth, and the truth will set you on the right path. Don't let your inability to see how you are going to achieve your true desire keep you from acknowledging what it really is. Make your desire a reality.

Here's another idea. When you are having difficulty discovering the desires inside yourself, just guess. You'd be surprised at how accurate a guess can be. Guessing can also open the door to a part of your heart that has been closed for some time.

One woman I know was stuck and just couldn't move forward. I asked her to guess what she desired most. She looked up at the ceiling and said, "Well, maybe it could be that I was closer to my son." Then she started to cry. That was her Core Desire.

Another man told me, "I just don't know what I want."

"Guess," I said.

He shrugged his shoulders and said, "It might be that I was involved with people more."

Then I asked, "If you were involved more with others, what would that give you?" The man got teary as he told me that his wife had passed away a few months ago, and he missed her terribly. He had found the only thing that helped ease the emptiness and loneliness was being with other people.

CLARITY BRINGS RESULTS

Core Desires can free you from staying mired in deep ruts and routines.

A Matter of Life and Death

Craig Newton is fifty-four years old and has been overweight most of his adult life. For the past ten years he has often fluctuated between 75 and 130 pounds above the recommended weight for men of his height and build. Craig's physical activities have been reduced drastically as a result of his excess weight, but the more damaging effect has been his lowered self-esteem. As he has grown older, the health consequences have increased. Despite his weight, he is proud of his family, his marriage, and his career accomplishments. He is financially comfortable and involved in community activities outside work and family life.

When I first met Craig, he told me, "Over the years, I've thought my life would be complete if I could overcome my addiction to food. This is difficult for me to rationalize, especially since I have been disciplined and successful in most other areas of my life. I have set goals to lose weight many times, I have tried many of the weight-loss programs with only short-term success, and I have sought psychological therapy with only limited success. In the end, the pleasure and satisfaction I receive from food has always prevailed.

"About two years ago, I started having some eyesight fluctuations. I went to the doctor and was diagnosed with early stages of type 2 diabetes. The complications of this disease were explained to me in graphic detail, and I was immediately put on diabetic medication and received counseling from a nutritionist about the necessity of following the diabetic exchange diet.

"This threat to my health scared me into better eating habits. I immediately realized the positive results. During the next three months, I was focused on doing everything I had to do to overcome this terrible, and possibly deadly, illness. As a result, I lost fifty pounds, brought my sugar levels under control, and reversed the symptoms I had experienced. The doctor was so pleased with my progress he discontinued the diabetic medication.

"Yet with the health threat gone, I quickly returned to my old habits—regaining most of the weight I lost. I know that I am sitting on a ticking time bomb and I must again regain control of my behavior or face the fact that the quality of my life will severely diminish. It will come down to which desire is stronger—food or life.

"I wanted with all my heart to avoid the serious problems of type 2 diabetes. The minute I was clear about these problems, I had the strength from inside to do what needed to be done. I was able to lose the fifty pounds again in just three months because I could identify the necessity to lose weight as a genuine Core Desire.

"Interestingly, I never wrote down any goal. I just had the Core Desire for the problem to go away. And it did. But once again, as soon as the symptoms disappeared and I had lost the weight, I began to repeat the cycle of dangerous behavior. I had proven that I could lose weight when it was a Core Desire to do so.

"I learned that 'shoulds' have no power to motivate. I have a Core Desire to live, and keep my eyesight, but no matter what my mind-set is, it isn't enough. My heart must be in it, or nothing will change—even after receiving a death threat.

"All the logical thinking, goal-setting, visualization, or affirmations in the world could not help me lose weight. Until losing weight became a 100 on my Core Desire Scale, the weight stayed on. Once I discovered my true desire to be healthy, nothing would stop me. I did whatever it took to lose the weight again and stay healthy for my family, and for me."

When Earning More Money Means a New Lease on Life

D. Scott Elder came to me realizing that over a period of years, there was still a big gap between where he was and where he wanted to go. He seemed to be stuck. When he learned about Core Desires, he knew he had found the answer he had been seeking. Only after understanding Core Desires did he discover that he truly wanted to be a public speaker.

"I set out with great enthusiasm and determination to achieve this desire. After encountering many obstacles, I decided I would start my own seminar company. Within two years, starting with no money and three like-minded partners, we built up one of the largest seminar companies in the world, earning fifty-five million dollars a year, teaching people how to invest in the stock market with the help, and tools, available on the Internet. Today my family and I enjoy a lifestyle that, at one time in my life, would have seemed totally impossible for me to achieve. I now know that anything is possible if it is a Core Desire."

Nathaniel Branden

"Living consciously means being present to what we are doing, while we are doing it. It means being eager to acquire information, knowledge, and feedback on our interests, values, goals, purposes, and projects. It means having self-awareness through self-examination. The less conscious we are, the more we operate mechanically, and the more restricted our options are in any situation. We may choose to ignore clear indicators that our strategies and tactics have become obsolete. The more conscious we are, the more options we see; therefore, the more effective and powerful we can be in responding to life's challenges. Your life is important. Honor and fight for your highest potential. People resign themselves to frustrations much too regularly. They often give up on their own lives much too readily, much too easily. They are too quick to draw very malevolent and drastic conclusions from one or two disappointments or failures."

Jack Canfield and Mark Victor Hansen

"The first principle of success is simply this: You have to figure out what you want in all areas of your life, including your health, happiness, relationships, and finances. Some obstacles are bigger than others and take longer to overcome. You can't do it all over a weekend. But you are only one good idea away from success, one good idea away from being rich, one good idea away from being healthy—and you make the decision. We have faced our own tough times, including a bankruptcy, so we understand being down. And we also know something about how to bounce back. The transition starts by getting into solitude, into the silence of the soul where you get to meet God face-to-face, so to speak. It is in that silence that you see who you are and what your purpose is in life."

PERSONAL EXAMPLES

When teaching my concepts, I often ask for volunteers so I can demonstrate that what I teach works—and works quickly. I relish the chance to conduct live demonstrations of what I have taught, as these dramatically reinforce the principles.

Matters of the Heart

At a seminar I conducted in Florida, there were about five hundred people in attendance. The minute I asked for volunteers, Elizabeth, a beautiful young lady in her late twenties, leaped out of her chair. She was anxious to learn about, and apply, her Core Desires.

"What would you like to have in your life that you are not getting?" I asked her.

Elizabeth first said she wanted financial independence. I asked the audience to measure her response on a scale of 1 to 100; the audience felt her desire was only between 40 and 60. Elizabeth was indignant and quite defensive. She stomped her foot on the stage and said, "How dare you tell me what I want! I really do want financial security!"

Even though she was emotional, Elizabeth was speaking from her head, not her heart.

My next question completely disarmed her. I asked, "If you had financial security, what would it give you that you don't have?" This time she didn't say anything. She did, however, quickly glance at the man who had been sitting next to her. I caught that very slight action and asked her if her Core Desire had anything to do with him. She nodded.

So I then invited her friend, Greg, to the stage and asked him if she could speak from her heart regarding her Core Desire, since it involved him. He gave his permission.

When I asked Elizabeth the same question a second time, she was silent; she just looked down at the floor. When she looked up, she was crying. "I just want him to set a date for our wedding," she said.

I immediately turned to the audience and asked them to measure that response. Everyone could see and feel the depth of her emotion. Marriage was definitely a 100 on her Core Desire Scale.

What had happened to the financial security Elizabeth said she wanted? In less than two minutes, her desire had changed.

When I asked Greg if he loved this woman, he quickly said, "Yes. With all my heart."

"Did you ask her to marry you?"

He again said, "Yes."

"Do you still want to marry her?"

He said, "Absolutely. She's the greatest, she's my best friend."

"How long have you been engaged?"

"Six years," he replied sheepishly.

"So, why haven't you set a date yet?"

Now it was Greg's turn to look down at the floor. When he raised his head to look at me—and the woman he loved—he said, with a quavering voice, "I'm afraid to set a date to get married until I can afford to take care of a wife and family."

I asked Elizabeth if she knew he felt that way. She said, "I had no idea."

I then asked her, "Would you still marry Greg, as broke as he is?"

"Yes. I would."

I then asked Greg if he knew Elizabeth would marry him even though he was broke. He was surprised, and speechless. He just shook his head as he fought back the tears. Greg's Core Desire, to keep from being embarrassed or feeling like a failure in the eyes of the woman he loved, was so strong that it had overridden his desire to marry Elizabeth.

Several months later I received a card from them telling me that they had married. All they needed was some help discovering their Core Desires and a little direction.

Money in the Bank

At a conference for banking professionals, I asked a volunteer to come to the stage. A man came up, saying he owned several banks and that his Core Desire was to increase cash flow.

> *"Throw your heart over the fence, and the rest will follow."*
>
> —Norman Vincent Peale

When I asked, "If you had more cash flow in your banks, what would that give you that you're not already getting?" he paused. He had to search deep in his heart to find the truth. Then he said, "More time."

I asked, "If you had more time, what would you do with it?" He told me that if his banks had greater cash flow, he could quit spending so much time at the office and do what he really wanted—teach at a university. He told us how much he loved working with young people and helping them succeed. He became so animated and emotional that we could easily tell that he had definitely found a 100 on his Core Desire Scale.

He had to accomplish three or four things to help increase cash flow and work toward becoming qualified to teach. Now that he had identified his Core Desire, he went right to work to make it a reality. Within a short period of time, he was teaching at his local college and said he was much happier.

What you might initially think is a Core Desire often isn't. You may have to dig deeper and ask the Search Question several times: "If I had_____, what would it give me that I am not getting?" This is how you drill down to your Core Desires. Don't let what you do today—no matter how good you are at it or how much money you make at it—be confused with what you want to do. They may be totally different. For maximum power and joy, always follow your heart.

Valerie Wilcox

When I first met Valerie, she was a corporate trainer. By asking herself the probing Core Desire Search Questions, she discovered that, even though she really liked speaking and training, what she wanted most to do was to write murder mysteries. That seemed like an off-the-wall idea—it was something she'd never done before, and it was unrelated to anything she had ever done in her life.

When Valerie finally discovered, and acknowledged, her Core Desire, her Conquering Force was unleashed and provided the courage and ability she needed. She didn't know how to go about writing mysteries to earn a living, but that didn't stop her—she was on the path.

Valerie recognized the power of the Conquering Force as soon as she felt it, but it took her a long time to follow her true passion. She had a hard time letting go of what others thought she should be doing with her education and work experience.

"I even convinced myself that my true Core Desire was doing what I'd always done—teaching and giving management development seminars. The problem was that I was very unhappy, especially when I discovered deep inside what I truly wanted to do with my life. When I finally got the courage (at almost fifty years old) to admit that I am a writer and always have been, everything changed. Following my true passion, my Core Desire, has opened more doors than I ever dreamed possible."

Michelle

When I met Michelle, she was in her fifties. She told me that her Core Desire was to travel. I asked her, "What else would you like to have, or do, that is a one hundred on the Core Desire Scale?"

"I don't know," she said.

"Guess," I said.

"I'd like to spend more time with my husband," she said. There was much more emotion in her face and voice.

"If you had the time, what would that give you that you don't have right now?" I asked.

She didn't know what to say. Then, in a faltering voice, she confessed that she really wished she and her husband were closer.

"If you were closer to your husband, what would that give you that you aren't getting?"

Whatever it was, it was definitely a 100 because she started to cry. It was such a huge emotional desire, it caused her deep feelings to surface. When she regained her composure, she said that she wanted, more than anything, to have a relationship with her husband that allowed her to feel safe and important. Safe to discuss her feelings, knowing they would be dealt with softly, and to feel that she really mattered to him. She didn't like feeling as if everything in his life came before her.

With this new understanding of her Core Desire, and some direction from me, she approached her husband and asked him to help her feel the way she wanted to feel. Was she afraid to talk with her husband about this? Yes, but she did it. The results were what she yearned for— he wanted to try to make her feel happy, he reassured her that he loved her, and he promised he would learn how to make her feel that she was, indeed, number one in his life.

Wheelchair Quarterback

A man in his early thirties was sitting in a wheelchair in the middle of the center aisle. He raised his hand and said, "I don't want to ruin your seminar or anything, but what you are teaching is a lie—at least it is for me. You say that if I discover my Core Desires and pursue them, I will eventually achieve them, right?"

"Yes," I said.

"Well, it won't work," he said, "at least not for me."

I knelt down beside him and asked, "What would you like to have, that is a one hundred on your Core Desire Scale? What aren't you getting right now in your life?"

With conviction he said, "I want to play pro football." Many in the audience thought this desire was a 100. I did not, so I asked him why he liked football. He told us that in high school he was an exceptional quarterback and broke local records. He was important, valuable, and popular. Many girls wanted to date him, and he was offered several scholarships by major universities. He went on to become one of the best quarterbacks in the history of that school, setting several records. The pros had scouted him, and he was expected to go high in the draft.

Then tragedy struck—he was involved in a major automobile accident, breaking his back and paralyzing him from the waist down. That was the end of his football career. Still, he enjoyed football vicariously—

he went to many games and watched all the games he could on TV. He knew the names, numbers, and statistics of all the major players.

As he was talking about his football experience, I paid close attention to his emotions. When he mentioned feeling important and being popular, I recognized that these were the real highlights of his football experience. I asked him, "What if I could help you feel as valuable, important, and popular as you felt when you played football?"

When he looked at me, I could easily tell that I had reached his heart, where all the genuine desire was. He dropped his head down, covered his eyes, and began to sob. "If you could do that for me, I would be eternally grateful," he said quietly.

His real Core Desire wasn't to play football. It was to have all the wonderful feelings that playing football had provided him. Since I had experienced all those feelings without playing football, I knew that it was possible.

When trying to discern your Core Desires, pay close attention to the responses and emotions elicited by the Search Question. You could overlook a key phrase, comment, or feeling if you are not careful. Emotions are not always easy to sense or detect.

Often people will answer the question flippantly, or without focus. Often I will hear a goal they have had for many years, and when I tell them it is not a 100 on the scale, they say things like "Okay, you want to know what I *really* want?" Then they say what is really in their heart and get right to the Core Desire. Sometimes they joke about a Core Desire—don't let this fool you. Oftentimes people joke about the things that are most important to them, because to get serious about it is quite painful. They joke around to hide the hurt.

In deciding whether something is a true Core Desire, pay attention to the words you use to describe it. If you use words like *probably, likely, maybe, possibly, perhaps,* or *I think,* what you're describing is not a Core Desire. Phrases like *I think, I should, I ought to, I need,* and *could be,* clearly indicate that what you're mulling over isn't a Core Desire. If you are reluctant to investigate what it will take to achieve your "want," it is not a Core Desire. If you feel that it is too much work, it isn't a Core Desire.

Procrastination comes from not wanting to do something or not knowing how to make it happen given your circumstances. Sometimes it is too painful to keep looking at what you really want but believe you can't ever have, so you never look at it. This doesn't make the feelings go away, it just pushes them deeper down into your heart. Your feelings get buried but still exhibit a measure of influence on your actions—and certainly limit your happiness.

Many people suffer anguish because they know what their Core Desires are, but they don't know how to get them. They just keep on doing things that don't work. They look for solutions somewhere "out there" rather than within their hearts. If you think that something outside you is the cause of your problems, you will look outside yourself for the answers.

Others think they know what they want but often find they are wrong. They work hard to get what they think they want, but they fail. And then they try again and again. Or they do all that work and spend all that energy and money to pursue what they think is a Core Desire, but when they obtain it, they still feel empty.

Marybeth

Marybeth came to me for advice regarding a specific personality trait that was creating serious marital problems. She knew she needed to change it. She had sought the advice of marital counselors, and each told her to read a specific book. When she came to me, I also recommended a specific book with insights regarding her problem. Marybeth dutifully bought all the recommended reading and placed the books on her nightstand—but she never read them.

Around this same time, Marybeth discovered she was pregnant with her first baby. She was so anxious, she couldn't wait—she wanted to be the best mother possible. So she bought several books about babies and parenting, read them all, and prepared for the day when her precious baby would make its debut into this world.

What was the difference between the two stacks of books? The first set fell under the category of "I should, I ought, or I need to change." These dutiful attitudes produced more guilt than action. The other stack represented something really exciting to Marybeth; she could hardly wait to read them. She even interviewed several parents to learn how they raised their children. This interest easily ranked 100 on the Core Desire Scale.

Excitedly and anxiously conducting an investigation and steeping yourself in knowledge is highly indicative of a Core Desire. Like a sleeping volcano, it certainly hasn't blown sky-high as yet, but the early warning rumbles are there if you know how and where to listen.

The stack of books about motherhood and babies were read thoroughly by Marybeth. Her desire to change her personality trait ranked much lower on her Core Desire Scale. It was powerful enough to ask experts for help and to invest money, but not enough to find the answers being sought—and work toward achieving them no matter what. That goal will never happen until it becomes a 100 on the scale. Her heart just isn't in it.

When we are pushed into doing something, we resist. But when it is a Core Desire, no pushing is necessary, and no resistance occurs. No one likes to be pushed into something they don't want to do.

Nike's famous motto "Just Do It" sounds great, but you will only "do it" if you want to do it. The willpower required to finish a task only exists if there is a Core Desire behind it. When a Core Desire is propelling you, your willpower is automatic—and success is assured.

YOU WILL SEE RESULTS

You can always tell when people are working toward a Core Desire by the results they achieve. When they are working on a Core Desire, they are enjoying themselves and are determined not to quit until they achieve their heart's desire. They are learning and doing the things they need to do to get what they want, even though they may get hurt, injured, or discouraged.

For example, two of my daughters love to snowboard. When they first hit the slopes, they fall down a lot. The next day they are so sore they can hardly walk, but they can't wait to go again. A dear friend of mine, a professional skier, damaged his knee severely. After having six pins put in his knee, having a cast on his leg from hip to ankle, he asked the doctor how long it would be before he could go skiing again. "Not this season," he was told. But my friend was up skiing—in his cast—in just six weeks! Even pain won't stop you when it's a Core Desire. It may slow you down, but it won't stop you.

When Henry Ford was asked what contributed most to his success, he said, "I keep my mind so busy thinking about what I want to accomplish that there's no room in it for thinking about the things I don't want." It's critical that you focus your time and energies only on the things you really, truly want—only on your Core Desires. It's quite easy to stay focused once you identify them, in spite of all the problems and hurdles in your path.

In the absence of a Core Desire, a nasty monster called Negative Labels lurks. When you fail at something, you tend to give yourself negative labels, such as "I don't have what it takes," "I'm not smart enough," "I'm too shy," or "I guess I didn't want it badly enough. It must not be a Core Desire."

You *are* smart enough to learn whatever you want to learn. It's not a matter of *can* you learn what it takes, it's a matter of do you *want* to learn it. When you want something enough, you will do whatever it takes for as long as it takes to get it.

Once you know what your Core Desires are, you will automatically work toward them because they become priorities. Core Desires are things you are always trying to do, and when you are pursuing the things you love in all areas of life, you will find the secret of peak achievement, balance, and happiness in life. Suddenly, astonishing sources of energy become available when you are pursuing your Core Desires.

Listening to your head while trying to determine your Core Desires will lead you off course. Your head usually makes decisions based on facts and data gathered from your own or others' personal experiences. Your mind can learn anything you want it to. The operative word is *want*. It can help you solve problems so you can achieve the desired end result. It can help you acquire traits, attitudes, and abilities you didn't have before.

To identify your Core Desires, pay close attention to your emotional reactions—they come from your heart. You must have the proper heart-set—not mind-set—to achieve your Core Desires. With practice, you'll develop the ability to evaluate whether what you are considering is a genuine Core Desire and whether you'll be willing to put forth the effort to achieve it. Learn to focus on your Core Desires so you don't waste time and money on other things.

Having a life in which *everything* you do is driven by Core Desires—things you love to do or to be—is the most satisfying and fulfilling way to live. When you embark on the journey to identify your Core Desires, you will open up a whole new way of living—a life where everything you ever wanted will be available to you or you will be on the path toward it—and loving it.

PART 2

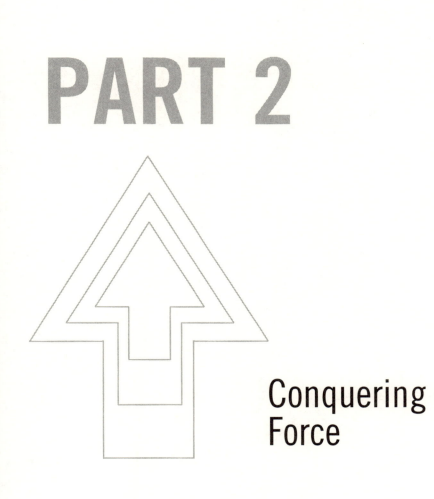

Conquering
Force

The Conquering Force Within You

There is a power under your control that is greater than poverty, greater than the lack of education, greater than all your fears and superstitions combined. It is the power to take possession of your own mind and direct it to whatever ends you may desire. — ANDREW CARNEGIE

here is an incredible energy and power within each of us just waiting to be unleashed by our Core Desires—I call it the *Conquering Force*.

To conquer is to get what we seek or overcome obstacles by physical, mental, or moral force. And force is the power to act effectively and to move against resistance. And so your Conquering Force is your innate ability to act effectively to get what you seek by overcoming all obstacles and resistance in your way. By tapping into the Conquering Force, we can achieve amazing results.

What portion of your "potential being" do you occupy? What part of your "soul's resources" do you use? Would you like to know the source of all success? Would you like to make better use of your resources; achieve what you most desire to

> "Most people live, whether physically, intellectually, or morally, in a very restricted circle of their potential being. They make use of a very small portion of their consciousness, and of their soul's resources in general."
> —William James

be, have, and do in life; and gain greater success and fulfillment in your life and work?

When you unleash the Conquering Force, you will achieve your Core Desires. Here's an example. When my wife wanted a piano, we bought, rebuilt, and refinished an old piano. It quickly became a beautiful and treasured piece of furniture. The only problem was that it didn't come with a bench. After searching to no avail for the right bench, my wife decided she'd just have to make one. She didn't know the first thing about making a piano bench, but it was a Core Desire. She really wanted a matching bench, with the same kind of carving on the legs, the same rich patina, and the same styling, even though the piano was over a hundred years old. So she signed up for a woodworking course at a local technical college. She learned how to use power saws, joiners, routers, drills, and wood lathes. She learned all about dowels, glues, carving, and wood finishes.

Within six weeks, her piano bench was born. It has since become a beautiful part of our home. By choosing just the right finish, she was able to match the piano in color, and the leg styling was an interpretation of that gracing the old piano.

The day she started to work on the bench, her gratification was instantaneous—because she was doing what she wanted. She enjoyed the whole process. She never said, "I hate to go down to the shop," or "This isn't any fun." Since the bench was a Core Desire, she simply drove to the shop each week and learned how to do what was needed. She was excited to do so—she could hardly wait to get there and find out what she didn't know. She enjoyed nearly every minute of it. The final product was a few weeks away, but there was constant gratification. When you pursue Core Desires, you gain gratification every step of the way because you are working toward an end result you really want.

There were things she didn't like about the bench-making process. She didn't enjoy the time she hurt her hand or got dirt and dark stains under her nails from the wood finish. She even ruined two bench legs and had to start over, but that setback didn't stop her. Her Core Desire was genuine, and it automatically kept her motivated.

When you identify and focus on your Core Desires, you unleash the Conquering Force—that potent, God-given force that causes everyone to accomplish everything and anything. Your past cannot control your future unless you let it.

CORE DESIRES IGNITE
THE CONQUERING FORCE

Core Desires are the ignition mechanism for the Conquering Force. This is what a Core Desire can do in your life—ignite the Conquering Force within you. I've taught hundreds of karate students, most of whom indicated they wanted to be black belts, but few of them ever achieved that distinction. Not because they didn't have the ability but because it wasn't a Core Desire. The sooner you identify your Core Desires, the sooner your Conquering Force kicks in. Then, and only then, will you truly have what it takes to achieve at high levels, which is where the greatest joy and happiness can be found.

This unstoppable Conquering Force already resides within you. Everything that you do, have, or become is a direct result of it. It is the reason you have achieved anything of significance to date—including learning to walk, talk, tie your shoes, drive a car, swim, ski, play an instrument, or sing. It is the reason we build houses, create computers, eradicate diseases, or put a man on the moon. Everything that you achieve, at any point in your life, serves as evidence that you already have Core Desires and the Conquering Force within you.

Although this Conquering Force is one of your greatest gifts, you are probably only vaguely aware of its powers; hence, you aren't using it as often as you could. When you tap into your Conquering Force, you can achieve your Core Desire in any area of your life.

The axiom "Use it or lose it" applies to the Conquering Force. You'll still have it, just as you'll always have your biceps, but its latent energy needs to be tapped. The electrical energy wired into the walls of your kitchen is there, but you tap into it only when you plug in and use an appliance. We all have an unlimited supply of

> "Intense desire creates not only its own opportunities but its own talents."
>
> —Eric Hoffer

latent energy that can be converted to kinetic energy the instant we plug into it by identifying our Core Desires.

Wally Amos

When Wally was forced out of his own cookie company, it seemed utterly unfair. But he refused to be a victim:

> When my company rejected me and gave me lemons, I decided to turn those lemons into lemonade. I remembered that doors had slammed in my face before, yet others had always opened to more brilliant prospects. I chose to see my current situation as the necessary impetus for creating a fabulous future. So I drew myself up and began to radiate a confident attitude. My intuition told me a divine plan was at work. I reminded myself that life is a process and that everything works together for the best. I came to a place of understanding which turned my heart right around. My suffering and rejection turned into a sense of comfort and peace.
>
> This acceptance recharged me and became a powerful force in my ensuing renewal. I decided not to give up, or complain, about what had happened—I refused to think that I was a failure. Rather, I threw aside all the negative beliefs I had been taught in my life and I began to explore the possibilities ahead. I managed to triumph over financial misfortune because I drew on the power within to turn a seemingly hopeless situation into an absolute winner.

You, too, can use the creative power of the Conquering Force to confront and shape your unique reality. You can love and enjoy everything that you do when your projects and experiences are an extension of yourself. Your Core Desires become a reality to the extent that you pour yourself into them. You will say along with Wally Amos, "I go out with a heart filled with passion and actualize what I desire. Everyone who achieves greatness or fulfillment in life starts out with a dream or desire and these call up limitless spiritual resources."

An unlimited power to create lies within you. When you act on your Core Desires, the outcome is often far grander than you might imagine. "Outcomes are often not what I expect," said Wally, "and yet I always find myself feeling completely satisfied with the way things work out. When you have faith in the outcome, no matter what it may be, you cannot stop yourself from living and working with enthusiasm. As I put what I feel into action, I am filled with vitality and happiness."

I once met a man who entered the Hawaiian Iron Man race, one of the toughest races ever devised. At seventy years old, he was the oldest entrant. As he was introduced, at a meeting with the company that sponsored him, the speaker said, "I'm forty-five years old, and I could never do what he is doing."

The athlete responded, "When I was your age I couldn't either." Amazingly, he hadn't started running until he was sixty-four years old.

Such latent ability lies within each of us. Some people constantly tap into their Conquering Force and use it to enhance and prolong their lives. When the late George Burns was asked if, given the chance, he would do anything in his life differently, he said, "Not really, I'd rather be a failure at something I love doing than to be successful at something I hate. I've always been in love with show business, and I still am. Show biz is and has always been my main desire."

Kevin Freiberg

"It is possible to go home at the end of the day emotionally charged. You will develop the courage, confidence, and contagious enthusiasms when you find a purpose you're crazy about. Inner strength and high self-esteem follow from having a strong sense of purpose and direction. We can rise to any height when we passionately believe that our lives are wrapped up in a cause that gives us a sense of meaning and significance. When we see how our efforts contribute to a larger cause, or a worthy purpose, we fulfill one of our deepest desires—the desire to make a difference. When we know that our lives, and our work, have meaning, we still have energy at the end of the day. Find a purpose you're crazy about, a purpose to which you are willing to give the totality of who you are, and who knows—you may recapture your idealism. You will regain a sense of adventure and playfulness, and turn routine into festivity."

Core Desires stimulate our senses and awaken our entrepreneurial spirit. They fuel our imagination, release our creative energy, and draw a deep sense of commitment to action. It's difficult to take action toward something you don't desire.

WHEN YOU HAVE IT AND WHEN YOU DON'T

How can you know when you are—or are not—tapping into the Conquering Force?

When You Don't Have It

When you are not tapping into the Conquering Force, you'll feel as if you're drifting like a stick in a river. Life will take you wherever it wants instead of you controlling where your life goes. You will set goals but never reach them, and you'll feel that life is ruling you. Maybe you'll even decide to accept the status quo, thinking you can't do anything about it. You may believe that you don't have any choices and end up accepting that you'll never achieve what you want in your life. Worse still, you may view your situation as hopeless—dying emotionally or spiritually because of your limiting paradigms. If any of these things are happening in your life, you haven't yet discovered that you do, indeed, have choices and can make changes. You were not born for mediocrity or unhappiness. Because of your ability to choose, you can control a lot more than you think.

When You Do

You will know the moment when you have tapped into your Conquering Force because you'll feel alert, alive, excited about your life, and you'll know you're in charge of what you're doing. You will be enjoying the path you are on. You can find a way to do what needs doing and get results. You'll go out and make things happen for yourself. Your indomitable spirit comes from your Conquering Force. You'll have a feeling of well-being and a sense of accomplishment. You'll be happy, even through the tough times. As you accomplish what you set out to do, you will be surrounded by both tangible and intangible evidence that you have unleashed your Conquering Force to achieve your Core Desires.

RELATED FORCES

Once you have discovered your Core Desires and unleashed the Conquering Force, ten other internal forces come into play: enthusiasm, joy, creativity, focus, drive, commitment, discipline, stamina, talent, and other resources.

Like cousins in a family, these forces are all closely related. Working together, they become synergistic and dynamic. Once you identify something you want badly enough, your mind automatically becomes more creative. You become enthusiastic, focused, committed, disciplined, and dedicated, and you make better use of your talents and other resources.

Tragically, most people don't know how to employ these forces. Through my own experience—and the vicarious experiences of countless others who have overcome difficulties, past histories, and seemingly insurmountable problems—I know that the ability to learn and perform is greatly enhanced when Core Desires trigger your Conquering Force.

If you put a 100-watt light bulb into a lamp, obviously you'll get more light than with a 25-watt bulb. So it is with the Conquering Force. Getting up in the morning and going to work may only be a 25 on the Core Desire Scale. However, you may come home at night and work at a furious pace until midnight to complete the boat you are building; this effort is at 100. It's an effort you enjoy, no matter how late the hour.

How can you judge how much power you're deriving from the Conquering Force? Use this "Power Meter" to rate yourself in each of these forces.

YOUR POWER METER			
Force	*How Do You Rate?*		
	Low	*Moderate*	*High*
Forces of the Heart *Enthusiasm, excitement, passion* *Happiness, joy, fun, play*	____ ____	____ ____	____ ____
Forces of the Mind *Creativity, innovative thinking* *Focus, concentration*	____ ____	____ ____	____ ____
Forces of the Will *Drive, determination* *Commitment, dedication* *Discipline, consistency* *Stamina, persistence, endurance*	____ ____ ____ ____	____ ____ ____ ____	____ ____ ____ ____
Forces of Resources *Talent, gifts, abilities* *Wise use of resources*	____ ____	____ ____	____ ____

There can still be some achievement even when the Conquering Force is seemingly dormant, because you always have some degree of desire. But if the Conquering Force is engaged at a very low level, you may never get out of bed. If the Conquering Force is engaged at a moderate level, you will do your duties—assigned tasks, shopping, and other items on the routine of your to-do list, if these are things you have to do. But when the forces of your heart, mind, and will are engaged at high levels, you will tap into amazing energy, passion, and power.

Moreover, other people can tap into the power of your Conquering Force for their own personal benefit—especially when their Core Desires are closely aligned with yours. In these instances, you will become a leader or mentor to those who want to follow your example, pursuing a similar path to progress in their lives and careers.

INTRINSIC MOTIVATION

When a person persists at a task, we say that person has determination or motivation. But where does that determination come from? Some would say it comes from dedication, commitment, or sense of duty. But I believe that Core Desires are the sole source of both the determination *and* the motivation that are critical for success. If you are not pursuing a Core Desire, you won't be very motivated or dedicated. You won't pursue something relentlessly *unless* it is a Core Desire.

Once you learn to unleash the power of your Conquering Force by drilling down to the Core Desires in all areas of your life, you will find your life filled with more joy, satisfaction, and balance. Notice that I said *learn*. Tapping into your Conquering Force happens automatically once you learn to correctly identify your Core Desires.

Motivation from the outside (extrinsic) usually only scratches the surface. That's why it has little or no lasting power. But when you're driven from within (intrinsic) by a Core Desire, nothing can stop you.

When you know exactly what you want, the Conquering Force becomes available to you at full strength. All great accomplishments are the result of extraordinary determination and drive, both of which come from Core Desires.

You, too, can become an extraordinary person—achieving *all* your heart's desires—when you harness your Conquering Force. It even creates new talents and characteristics as needed. The Conquering Force engenders enthusiasm, determination, commitment, creativity, discipline, and drive, and it leads to great satisfaction and joy. Any person who is in the process of achieving a Core Desire is already an extraordinary person.

I'm often asked, "What motivates you?" My

> "This creative power becomes available only when we are in that state of mind in which we know exactly what we want, and are fully determined not to quit until we get it."
> —Alexander Graham Bell

> "A wise man will make more opportunity than he finds."
>
> —Francis Bacon

answer is simple—I'm motivated from within by my many Core Desires. I clearly recognize my Core Desires, and then I act upon them because doing so brings me great rewards and joy. My Core Desires are written on my heart, and what is written on the heart always comes to pass.

A man once told me, "I don't understand how I can be something that I'm not or do something I'm not comfortable doing. I'm not confident, I'm not dynamic—I'm just a low guy on the totem pole. I can't take advantage of opportunities that come my way. How can I make the kind of money I want and need when I can't even earn enough to pay all my bills every month? In the past, I've never earned more than thirty-two thousand a year, and I'm limited because I don't have a master's degree." His list of reasons why he couldn't be more successful or earn more money was never-ending.

I asked him why he was letting his past determine his future. He couldn't answer, so I continued by talking about Core Desires and the Conquering Force. But he confessed that he had no hope and no chance because all the good opportunities had already passed him by. He felt his life was devoid of all happiness and joy.

Many people think opportunity only knocks once; others believe it knocks many times. But I say that opportunity doesn't knock at all. You must knock. When you are driven by a Core Desire, your Conquering Force won't allow you to knock lightly or timidly. You're anxious to get that door open because you want what's behind it, so you knock hard—with force and determination—until the door opens. You might even break the door down or pick the lock—you'll do whatever it takes to create the opportunity.

THE SERENDIPITY FACTOR

Incredible things happen independently of those you personally create. I call these serendipitous blessings. When you're pushing hard on door A, someone or something opens door B. Often, when you look through door B, what's behind it is much better than what you were going after in the first place. However, you wouldn't have seen door B open if you hadn't been in the hall pushing on door A. Get in the here and now and look for the other opened doors, or go open some doors on your own.

> "A strong desire for any object will ensure success, for the desire of the end will point the means."
>
> —William Hazlitt

When you learn to tap into your Conquering Force at full power, achievement and success are a foregone conclusion.

Tiger Woods's father, Earl Woods, said, "I never asked him to practice." At the tender age of two, Tiger had memorized his father's work number and would call him to ask if he could practice with him that day. This love affair with golf was no weak flame. Tiger said that he was fascinated with golf because his father seemed to enjoy it so much. Tiger's amazing success came from his Core Desire to play golf.

In Aikido expert Tom Crum's book, *The Magic of Conflict*, we are taught that if someone tries to punch you, you don't try to block the punch but rather use the energy from the punch to your own advantage. When you try to block a punch, you are using your power and strength to resist the other person. This sets up a win-lose confrontation. In Aikido, your strategy is to step aside with an accepting and pivoting movement, using the attacker's energy to throw him, or to apply a neutralizing technique. The key, as Tom teaches it, is to learn how to be centered, with both mind and body relaxed and alert. In this state of heightened awareness and connectedness, you stop thinking about mechanics and start to go with the flow of energy.

Centering yourself means gathering all your energy and focusing it on your physical center. When you are centered, you are also connected to a universal energy. You use adversities as opportunities to learn, grow, and move forward in your life. If you respond to events in a centered way, you will remain positive and progressive, keeping your energy and perspective focused on your Core Desires. If you are not cen-

> "Look not mournfully at the past. It comes not back again. Wisely improve the present. It is thine."
>
> —Henry Wadsworth Longfellow

tered, you are easily knocked off balance in tough times, responding negatively to everything that happens and with a tendency to take adversity personally.

Core Desires seem to give a person superhuman power to destroy all barriers and obstacles and achieve. When you are pursuing your heart's desire, you will remain centered—physically, mentally, and spiritually.

> *"The starting point of all achievement is desire. Weak desires bring weak results, just as small amounts of fire make a small amount of heat. When your desires are strong enough you appear to possess superhuman powers to achieve."*
>
> —Napoleon Hill

The Success Attitude

*There is no duty we so much underrate as the
duty of being happy.*
—ROBERT LOUIS STEVENSON

The **Success Attitude formula** makes achieving your Core
Desires simple. We all use this formula to reach our objectives,
whether we know it or not. It has been an integral part of my own
achievement experience.

The Success Attitude formula shows you how to unlock and open
the door of opportunity. Many people have listened to experts or
read their books and have been all fired up with that can-do
approach. But soon the fire goes out and they never get going, they
never take the first step, or they quit too easily. This won't happen
when you know your genuine Core Desires and apply the Success
Attitude formula.

$$SA = (CD + D) \times PA + P$$

Success Attitude = (Core Desires + Direction) × Proper Action +
Persistence

SUCCESS ATTITUDE

A Success Attitude is a frame of mind that allows you to accomplish whatever you want because you *know* that you can create the opportunity and then make it happen. You may not necessarily know *how* you will create the opportunity, you just know that you have the *ability* to learn whatever it takes to acquire the attributes, skills, and characteristics needed. With this foundation, you need only identify what you really want to learn about and then find a mentor to shorten your learning curve.

Remember that you are smart enough to learn whatever someone is willing to teach you. With the skill and attitude you learn from a mentor, you can then create the opportunity and make it happen. You may surprise yourself with the things you can do. You will acquire the talent and attitudes needed thanks to your Core Desires and your Conquering Force.

When you have faith and confidence in yourself, you will do more and attempt to do more. The ancient Greeks defined *faith* as "action out of confidence." The more confidence you have, the more action you will take.

Where can you get more faith and confidence? You can borrow it from someone who has plenty of it—from those who are already successful at whatever you want to learn—whether it's skiing, swimming, marriage, or business. When you apply what they have taught you, you will achieve the results as promised, thus greatly increasing your faith. When you exercise your faith, you will become a more confident and faith-full person.

CORE DESIRES

Use those strong, powerful, and heartfelt desires—those that measure 100 on the Core Desire Scale—to succeed at anything. Find the overwhelming, overarching desire that is so strong it will tap into the Conquering Force. The only thing that will cause you to do what is unfamiliar, uncomfortable, or even scary is knowing it is worth it. Your comfort zone is what you have right now in your life. If you want more out of your life, you must move into the discomfort zone—a much larger circle. The longer you stay in the discomfort zone, the more comfortable you become. Before long, the perimeter of the first circle disappears and your comfort zone will encompass this new, larger circle.

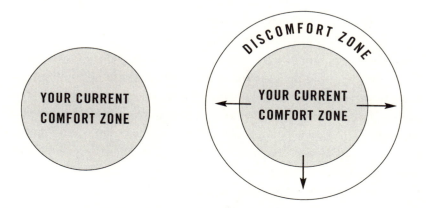

How large would you like your comfort zone to be? It can be as big as you'd like. You can choose to place no limits on yourself. If you can learn, you can do, have, or become whatever you want.

When I ask people, "How are *you* creating opportunity?" I hear many excuses. I have a rebuttal for each excuse—I've used them all myself. But what it really comes down to is, do you want it or not? If a person says he would like to learn to swim but is afraid of water, my response is very objective: Do you want to learn to swim or not? It's your choice. If the desire is big enough, you will do it even if the fear is there. It is that simple. Our limiting paradigms are what make it seem so hard.

Once, a woman timidly approached me and told me that she really wanted to take a job but was concerned that she wasn't "cut out for that kind of work."

"When you were cut out, what were you cut out for?" I asked.

She saw herself as "just a housewife."

When I ask people, "What are you?" I hear such things as "I'm just a secretary," "just a truck driver," "just a plumber," "just a mom."

"The person who says it can't be done should not interrupt the person doing it."

—Chinese proverb

People label themselves as "just-a." This "just-a" attitude is a way of downplaying your current roles. If you aren't happy in your current roles, you can change them. Everyone is "just-a" *human being* with all the abilities and attributes God gave us at birth. We can do, have, or become whatever our hearts desire. The potential of any human being is immense.

There will always be those who tell you "it can't be done." Some people—out of love or concern—may advise you not to move forward based on their opinion and limited experience. Without fail, those people who advise against breaking out of a rut and paint scary pictures of failure have never been successful on their own. Remind yourself not to listen to negative people who have never accomplished what you intend to do. People cannot bring you to a level they have never achieved—they can't teach you what they do not know themselves. But they sure can be discouraging.

I know a man whose parents had been wage earners their entire lives. Out of love and concern for their son, they tried to discourage him from going into business for himself. They'd tell him, "You won't have a steady paycheck." And when that didn't work, they'd tell him, "You know, eighty percent of all businesses fail. You won't have much of a chance. You don't have enough education. Get a good job, stay with a company, and work your way up."

The man didn't listen to his parents, or to anyone who cast doubt on his Core Desire. Today he is very successful, and glad he only listened to those who had already achieved what he wanted. The people that helped him get to their level are the ones who knew the way.

I was that young man, and I owe all my success to my Core Desires, my mentors, God, and an encouraging and supportive wife. My parents' paradigm about business and education may have been accurate, but to allow my past to control my future was ridiculous. My parents did not factor in the power of my Core Desires. They had never been in business for themselves, and their mind-set was limited to their personal experiences.

DIRECTION

Still, a Core Desire by itself won't get you where you want to go. If you live in California and want to drive to Washington, D.C., you may have a great desire, but you still need direction.

We already know that the shortest distance between two points is a straight line. Wouldn't it make sense to go straight, or as straight as possible, toward our desired objective? Identifying Core Desires has a way of making you want to fulfill them as quickly as possible. Yet many folks, after they've pinpointed their Core Desires, get bogged down because they can't find direction. So find an accurate map, trace the best route, check with the travel club, and find out about any detours. Minimize your delays and annoyances.

It may not be simple to map out *exactly* how you'll increase your income, increase your free time, overcome habits that hold you back, or create close relationships. It's always much harder to find a map for those—but they do exist.

Once you know what your Core Desires are, you can make use of tools that are available to you, such as the ones listed below. But remember, these tools alone—without Core Desires—will get you nowhere fast.

➡ *Mentors*

Throughout history, world leaders have had their mentors. Franklin Roosevelt had George Marshall; the King of England had Winston Churchill; Julius Caesar had Mark Antony. If people at the very top are smart enough to seek out and utilize mentors, don't you think we'd be smart to do the same thing?

➡ *Books*

For every Core Desire you have, you can find a book. When you read books that address your Core Desire, reading can be a joy and a pleasure. You'll devour the words and eagerly apply all you've learned. (That's your Conquering Force in action.) Interestingly, the Conquering Force eliminates boredom, because you're always doing what you want. Only buy books that pertain to your identified Core Desires.

→ *Audio and video programs*

There are many audio- and videotapes out there, about everything from taxes to relationships. If they apply to your Core Desires, these tapes can help you apply your Conquering Force effectively. Many programs provide specific how-tos. If the content pertains to your Core Desires, the message can be life-changing.

→ *Personal development courses and seminars*

Again, as long as the content pertains to one or more of your Core Desires, seminar presentations can help you achieve your desires. Many seminars are free or very inexpensive because local universities or other organizations sponsor them. Seminars and courses are among the most powerful and helpful experiences you can have. Some last an hour or two, some five days. Often they are very intense and they are generally designed to help you overcome personal obstacles hindering your growth and limiting your happiness. In these seminars and courses, you participate on an emotional level. My deepest Core Desire has always been to have the best relationship possible with my wife and children. Anything that can help me do that automatically helps me achieve my Core Desire.

PROPER ACTION

Without proper action, you can't obtain your Core Desires. A Latin proverb says, "If there is no wind, row." I add, "Row with *both* oars, but first untie the boat from the dock." The Conquering Force is the power that causes you to take the proper steps, no matter what the risk or how many obstacles you encounter.

Wanting to go to Washington, D.C., and simply selecting the route won't get you there. You've taken some action by reading about all the things to see; you've bought a map and done some calculations, but it isn't enough. You still must get in the car, fill it with gas, and take off. Without the map, you could have a difficult time getting there. Maybe you'd still get lost or get a flat tire. There are always risks associated with any journey, but the potential for problems doesn't stop you from trying, because it's a Core Desire to go on vacation and see the nation's capital.

This attitude of not letting risks and possible problems stop you applies to every area of your life. When you are working toward a genuine Core Desire, fear is not a limiting factor. If you are afraid to do something but do it anyway, does that mean that you are afraid or brave? The answer is both, but it's the Core Desires that make the fear manageable.

My wife and I decided to go to Vail, Colorado, with our two teenage daughters to hike in the Rocky Mountains. It was a beautiful summer day when we parked the car at the lodge and started off hiking. Right away my daughters saw that we could take one of the ski lifts and ride to the top of the mountain to take in the spectacular views.

When they asked if we could take the chair lift, my chest tightened. I'm afraid of heights. Those chair lifts go so high above the ground, and with nothing between me and a long fall but those tiny wooden slats to sit on, I said "Uh-uh." They told me that it was impossible to fall—millions of people ride these lifts with no accidents.

They pleaded, "Please, please, Daddy? It will be beautiful up there."

Because my Core Desire was to please my daughters and to have a wonderful experience with them, I took the chair lift to the top.

Was I scared? Absolutely. I was terrified. But I did it anyway, thanks to my Conquering Force.

Be careful not to confuse hard work with proper action. There are millions of hardworking people who have never enjoyed the pleasures of focusing on and living with the success of attaining genuine Core Desires. Some people say the harder you work the luckier you get. But when you are doing the right work, you get even luckier. Many people spin their wheels, producing a lot of action and effort but no real results. They keep working and staying busy but never seem to get ahead. Because they keep doing what they have always done, their lives stay the same.

PERSISTENCE

In your journey from your home in California to the Smithsonian Institute in Washington, D.C., you already have the direction you need and are taking proper action as you start the drive. Still, without persistence, you won't make it. After all, it's a long drive, and very real and valid obstacles can keep you from getting there. But if you really want to get there, if it is a Core Desire, you will do what is necessary.

If going to the Smithsonian is a 100 on your Core Desire Scale, you will find a way to get there—even if you are out of money and your car has broken down. You will find a way. Persistence is automatic when you have identified a Core Desire.

In the pursuit of Core Desires, you may not hit the bull's-eye on the first shot. You may have to take several shots and then learn to make adjustments. I failed in four different businesses before I achieved the level of success—and income—I now enjoy. Why did I keep starting over? Because I wanted to be free—and not just financially. I wanted to be my own boss and be in control of my time and money. Had I quit, as so many well-meaning people advised me to do, I wouldn't be free to come and go as I wish, nor would I be speaking to, and helping, people all around the world.

Almost all karate students have a tough time learning the hardest kick—the rear kick. It's so difficult because your body does not easily allow you to kick backward. Students who are just learning this kick have a hard time; they kick only about ankle or knee high and without proper form. After three or four lessons, they still have difficulty. They moan in frustration "I'll never be any good at this," "I'll never learn this kick." But when asked if they really want to learn it, they always say yes.

After I teach the motions necessary to master this kick, I give my students homework: practice the kick with each leg a thousand times a week for at least two weeks. I can usually tell who will become proficient at the kick by their reaction to

> "That which we persist in doing becomes easier to do, not that the nature of the thing itself has changed, but that our ability to do has increased."
>
> —Heber J. Grant

my instructions. Some agree to do the exercise, others protest, and still others persist. Those who persist become experts at the rear kick. All have the ability, but only a few have the heart-set.

After seeing the Success Attitude formula in action over the years, I'm convinced that it works every time. It will produce tremendous results and never fails. By following these simple steps, you can enjoy life at high levels of harmony, satisfaction, and joy. By following the Success Attitude formula, you will benefit greatly.

Mark Lesicka

In 1986 Mark was asked to make a donation to the Children's Hospital fund-raiser. The woman calling on behalf of the hospital told Mark a story about how her child had been cared for in a time of illness. Mark was so touched by the woman's story, he felt compelled to do all he could to make this fund-raiser a resounding success. He wasn't sure how he would do it; he only knew that it was important.

A few days later Mark was visiting one of several video stores he owns. The store manager told him about an article she had read about the Batmobile. She asked Mark if it would be possible to use the car as a promotional tool. At first Mark laughed, but then he thought immediately of the Children's Hospital fund-raiser.

After many calls to the rare car dealership nearby, Mark was able to convince the owner to donate the use of the Batmobile for the fund-raiser, with the stipulation that Mark pay for the advertising and transportation costs, as well as arrange permissions from Warner Brothers. The dealership also requested that any ads make it known that the car was being donated specifically for the Children's Hospital.

Mark set to work, securing the help of employees and friends. When he contacted the movie studio, he was surprised to learn that this was not the first time the Batmobile had been used in a fund-raiser. And he was pleased to learn that the studio would cover any insurance fees. Next Mark contracted with an agency to draw up an advertisement for the Batmobile. While the final ad was being constructed,

> "Vitality shows not only in the ability to persist but the ability to start over."
> —F. Scott Fitzgerald

> "The secret of success is constancy of purpose."
>
> —Benjamin Disraeli

Mark left for a short vacation. While on vacation, he received a call from his office saying that the dealership was calling the deal off. It seemed that the advertising agency had somehow failed to mention the Children's Hospital fund-raiser in the ad. Mark immediately called the dealership and promised to correct the advertisement.

Despite the obstacles in his way, Mark was driven by the Core Desire to help raise money for a cause he felt close to. The use of the Batmobile was a huge success—over four thousand people attended the event and, in just two days, raised 10 percent of the funds that were raised that year. Mark received numerous calls from other local hospitals requesting that the Batmobile pay visits to their fund-raisers and visit terminally ill children.

Because Mark was driven to help raise as much money as possible for the hospital, nothing stood in his way. Without ever writing down goals or making affirmations, he overcame obstacles, pursued all avenues, and ultimately persevered in the face of adversity. Once he had identified his Core Desire, his Conquering Force kicked into gear—and anything was possible.

Heber J. Grant

When Heber J. Grant was a boy, he joined a baseball club. He lacked the physical strength to throw the ball from one base to another or hit the ball or run well. He was teased and called "sissy." This painful teasing caused him to make a solemn vow to play on the best team and win the state championship. He bought a baseball and spent hours and hours throwing it against a barn. His arm would ache so badly he could hardly sleep at night. But he kept on practicing and eventually played on the team that won the state championship.

Steve Young

"In many ways I'm not a likely candidate to be a quarterback in the NFL. For starters, I harbored a lot of self-doubt for years. I was like

The Little Train That Couldn't. I kept saying, 'I can't do it. I can't do it.' So the secret to my success is just that I knew I had the ability and desire—deep down—and I held on. It seemed like success happened to me. I sat there in a 3-D game, and it kept coming at me. I just kept going ahead, kept improving my game, and somehow never stopped. I just took it a day at a time. And over time, I became *The Little Train That Could*. My new message to myself is 'I think I can. I think I can.' I overcame my doubts. Somehow you get things done that you never thought you could when you just move forward and hold on. The hard part was waiting behind Joe Montana. When I finally got my chance, the scrutiny was intense. I faced incredible odds. But I was drawn to the challenge. I kept saying, 'I'm sticking this one out. I want to see where it goes.' And one day I woke up as MVP of the league."

This level of persistence exists in all of us if we want something with *all* our heart. One of my mentors once taught me a lesson on adversity when he asked me what makes a kite fly. I said, "It's *the wind*." He said, "The answer is, the string. What would happen if, while flying a kite, you let go of the string? The kite would fall. You see, it's that resistance to the wind, provided by the string, that not only keeps it aloft but causes it to soar to great heights."

So when you encounter resistance or adversity, remember that you're like a kite flying in the sky and you need resistance to become strong and to stay up there or soar higher. I know that's true for me. As a result of seemingly negative things that have happened to me, I am where I am today. I sure didn't like them when they were happening, but hindsight shows that these experiences were some of the best things that could have happened to me.

The ability to solve problems is one of the most important elements of achievement in any endeavor. Problems will crop up. Accept that as a fact of life. Solving them is the way to succeed.

> "Perseverance is not a long race. It is many short races, one after another."
> —Walter Elliott

The Special Force of Mentoring

Hitch your wagon to a star.
— RALPH WALDO EMERSON

Having a mentor is an integral part of getting where you want to go and achieving what you want to achieve, as fast as possible, with the fewest mistakes. I consider mentors to be key components of maximizing your Conquering Force.

In your life, you have probably already enjoyed the help of several mentors. For example, you may have had a parent, coach, teacher, or associate who made a major impact on your life. A mentor could even be someone you don't know personally—someone whose philosophy or example touched you so deeply you decided to emulate him or her. In some way, directly or indirectly, these people were there for you. They knew what they were talking about, and they showed you a better way to achieve.

Why try to reinvent the wheel when you can talk to its inventor? The person who desires to be successful will always learn from other people's successes as well as from their mistakes.

> *"The important thing is to not stop asking questions."*
>
> —Albert Einstein

Everyone needs mentors. They are critical in our quest to enjoy the best our lives have to offer. Mentors are ideal if you want to capitalize on the shortcuts and proven methodologies for creating wealth, closer relationships, or any other important objective. Don't ever believe that someone made it to the top without the help of others. And don't let fear or pride keep you from seeking mentors.

> *"He who asks is a fool for five minutes, but he who does not ask remains a fool forever."*
>
> —Chinese proverb

A decade ago, mentoring was a hot buzzword—people acted as if it were something new—but mentoring isn't new in education or business. For centuries craftspeople have set up guilds with apprenticeship programs where newcomers learn their skills from seasoned artisans. Mentoring has been a mainstay in the world's military establishments: armies take in raw recruits and mold them into soldiers by using seasoned, experienced, and often battle-hardened drill sergeants as teachers. When recruits have classroom instructions, read textbooks, follow lesson plans, and use teaching aids, they are benefiting from the expertise of top military mentors.

Today, businesses also rely heavily on mentoring. Mentoring goes on every day, everywhere. It goes by many names, and it has made many advances. It is a source of guidance you should not leave to chance. Never ask someone to teach, train, guide, or lead you if that person has never successfully done what you want to do.

FINDING THE RIGHT MENTOR

Of whom are you going to ask questions? Obviously you'll seek someone who knows the answers. Whom you put your trust in is very important, so choose carefully. Seek the advice and guidance you need only from people who have achieved what you want to achieve.

There is a joke I once heard about two friends discussing religion. Call them James and Joe. James said to Joe, "Obviously you don't know anything about the subject."

"Sometimes we may
learn more from a
man's errors than his
virtues."

—Henry Wadsworth
Longfellow

"Yes I do," Joe retorted.

To prove that Joe didn't know anything about religion, James said he would give him five dollars if he could quote any of the Ten Commandments.

Joe accepted the challenge, thought long and hard, and then said, "Now I lay me down to sleep, I pray the Lord my soul to keep. If I should die before I wake, I pray the Lord my soul to take."

James was very surprised and handed Joe the money. "I didn't think you could do it!" he said.

You must be careful from whom you seek advice. Avoid those who only have opinions, not facts.

The importance of finding and utilizing a knowledgeable, experienced mentor is immeasurable. Usually it is not difficult to find a good mentor. Most highly successful people are more than willing to spend time with you and help you understand what got them there. Usually they love what they are doing, and if you share their enthusiasm for their specialty, they are willing to help. I know I am when someone asks me.

When I'm mentoring, I'm giving back that which was so graciously given to me. I love mentoring others and showing them how to create the success I now enjoy. I mentor others willingly because I love knowing that I played a part in their success. The sign of a good teacher is when the student surpasses the teacher.

People sometimes come to my office and stay for a week at a time. They fly with me on business trips or attend my speaking engagements. I even mentor over the telephone, via e-mail, and through newsletters—internationally. I became who and what I am because of my Core Desires to succeed, and because I asked successful people how they got where they are. Then I listened to what they said and did what they suggested.

"Smart people learn from experience. Super smart people learn from other people's experience."

—John Bytheway

In my office I have a plaque listing all the people who greatly affected my life. At the top of the plaque I engraved, "To these people I owe an eternal debt of gratitude for their substantial influence in my life." Each day when I sit in my office, I think of all the people who helped me get where I am today.

How do you get someone to mentor you? Simply ask. You can call them or write a letter. All you need to do is let your potential mentor know that you are serious and not interested in wasting their time. Let your prospective mentor know that you consider him or her to be the perfect role model for you. Give honest praise for their accomplishments, but more importantly, be sincere in your request and your dedication.

> "I like to listen. I have learned a great deal from listening carefully. Most people never listen."
>
> —Ernest Hemingway

When I was twenty-eight years old, I asked a wealthy gentleman from my church to mentor me. He had the kind of life I wanted—time for his family and plenty of money. Although I didn't know him, I called him and told him that I wanted to be like him and have the lifestyle he enjoyed.

He chuckled and said, "Sure! Come over to my house sometime, and I will tell you what I know." He was my first business mentor. I was able to create a substantial net worth over the next five years because of what he shared with me. I was a good student: I took notes in his presence, and I was an avid listener.

I find that many people are more interested in impressing their mentors than in listening to them. Taking notes or recording what your mentor says on tape will ensure that you don't overlook something important. It will also give you the chance to review your notes and listen to the tapes as needed.

Don't expect mentors to pop out of the woodwork and present themselves to you—seek them out. Networking is a great way to meet mentors. I have always found that when you are most in need of a teacher or mentor, one will enter your life. Don't stop with one mentor—seek many more. The time and effort you put into finding great mentors will be repaid many times in the long run. They'll prevent you from making time-consuming and costly mistakes. You may only get one good idea from a mentor, but it could be the very idea you need at the time.

"Judge Judy" Sheindlin

"When I was four years old, I was enrolled at a dancing school. I studied ballet, tap, and acrobatics—even though I didn't exactly fly through the air with the greatest of ease. After a fairly severe injury, I was excused from dancing classes until I could bring a note from the doctor. My parents were smart enough to realize that perhaps dance and acrobatics weren't for me. And I was allowed to gracefully withdraw from dancing school.

"From my experience, I believe that you must find and cultivate the few things a particular child is naturally good at from the beginning. In this way, you provide your children with the confidence to take healthy risks and to learn on their own. Over time, my parents came to realize that I had strong communication skills and a gift for languages, but I showed no flair for math or science—I got through those subjects with difficulty. But as a result of my parents' understanding, I was able to view myself as a successful orator, instead of a mediocre mathematician—an engaging communicator, instead of a failed ballerina. A child can learn more in a moment of success than can ever be learned in a month of failures."

Lou Tice

"Most successful people have benefited from a relationship with someone who served as a mentor to them. Generally, there are three factors that make a mentor credible to us. First, the mentor is like us in a significant way. Second, he or she has achieved a measure of personal success in a relevant field. Finally, he or she has mentored or coached others to success in that field. We can hold up the most admirable models, the highest quality benchmarks, and we can say to our children or to our employees, 'Here, look at this, and be like this.' But if we can't see ourselves being and doing those things, if the examples we set aren't assimilated, no lasting change will result.

"The best mentors are people who can see more in you than you can see yourself. They see you not only as you are, but also as you could be. They don't focus on your mistakes and shortcomings. Rather, they describe to you, frequently and vividly, your strength, power, and potential. Because they are credible, you give sanction to their vision. Over time, you develop a new internal standard. You say, 'Yes, that's me. I am like that,' and you act accordingly. Mentors are so convinced that you have greatness in you—their vision of what is possible for you is so clear and powerful—that they convince you, too. People naturally move in the direction of praise—away from harsh criticism. True mentors give you enhanced self-esteem and self-efficacy."

Colin Powell

"Do you enjoy sports and the strenuous life? Do you delight in overcoming obstacles, solving problems, and fixing things? Do you have a passion for excellence and a healthy desire to succeed? Do you have integrity and a sense of personal honor? Are you strong enough to be gentle? If you are that kind of person, then you are eligible for one of the most richly rewarding challenges that life can offer—mentoring a child. Children need positive adult role models. The more good role models they have, the better their chances of growing up into successful and contributing adult members of society. Mentored youth are 46 percent less likely to abuse drugs than those without mentors are. Mentored youth also get better grades. Mentoring is good for kids and for the whole community. We need more mentors, and we urgently need more people to take on the challenge of mentoring. Our youth, especially those who are growing up without fathers and mothers at home, need good role models.

"You will get as much back from serving others as you give. Serving makes you feel good about yourself while making a difference in someone else's life. More than that, giving back improves your own self-confidence and self-esteem, gives you a chance to learn new skills, and allows you to be a leader. Some men and women have discovered talents they never knew they had and have even found their life's work through serving others.

"You are a vital resource in, and for, your community. Reach out to other people to make their lives better and help point them in the right direction. Your energy, your idealism, and your commitment will help fulfill the promise of all our citizens."

LEARN THE LESSONS WELL

When you talk with mentors, ask them very specific questions—not just about the big picture but about little things, too. I remember talking before a sales organization and was astounded to learn that one of their salespeople had more than quadrupled an old sales record in one day—she had sold twenty-eight people on taking a specific course, which cost four hundred dollars—and not one of her colleagues had ever asked her to tell them how she did it!

I suggested that anyone who wanted to become as successful as she should talk with her about how she achieved such success. Ask about the details. Did she do any group presentations? If so, how did she set them up? Did she joke with her prospects? Did she meet them personally, or did she do it all over the telephone?

If you wanted to perform at the same level as this woman, you would do what she did, say what she said, and be like her. By asking mentors questions, you'll gain new insights and prove that you really want to learn all you can from them.

Note, however, that many successful people, particularly salespeople who are peak performers—accumulating accolades and awards—simply cannot explain what they do and how they do it to others. All their secrets remain locked up inside them. It isn't that they're unwilling to share but rather that they lack the ability to do so. Despite their level of success, these people simply don't have the skills to mentor.

My mentors have taught me many valuable lessons. For instance, when I take out a pen to write a note or sign contracts, I use a Mont Blanc, not a Bic. One costs $125, and the other costs 49¢. Both pens write well, but one makes a statement about your success, and when signing contracts with clients, image is very important. Making the right statement gives others confidence in me. I also wear a nice watch in business settings because my mentor told me that wearing a nice watch makes a statement about your success.

Another mentor taught me to always carry a hundred-dollar bill. It may seem silly, but you'll find you have an improved attitude when you have a hundred dollars in your pocket.

My wife and I have an unusually strong, close family, and we have raised five well-behaved children. Having such a family was a genuine Core Desire for us both, and so we sought out wise mentors. We interviewed several parents who had, in our opinion, raised exemplary children. We asked them how they did it, and they willingly shared their viewpoints and belief systems. They even provided us with specific parenting methods. For instance, one couple taught us that spanking children isn't necessary to discipline them. Another couple, with nine children under the age of fourteen, taught us how to get our children to be reverent and quiet in church. We applied what they taught us and found that it worked.

Don't hesitate to ask others to teach you what you want to know—in any area of life. By replicating their methods and attitudes, you'll get similar results. Finding and working with a mentor should be fun, easy, and very productive—you need not fly through life by the seat of your pants.

TIPS FOR BEING MENTORED

➡ *Select mentors who have successful experience in areas that you don't.*

You want to capitalize on their strengths and minimize your weaknesses and shortcomings. They must have achieved a high level of success in the same field, endeavor, or area that you are seeking to succeed in. You'll want someone who can challenge you and hold you accountable. You may have several mentors at one time. In fact, I recommend it. If you really think about it, you probably already have several mentors.

➡ *Find mentors who are willing, able, enthusiastic, compatible, and interested in mentoring you.*

You want someone you can talk with easily and comfortably. Some mentoring prospects will reject your requests, so you should be willing to reject those who just don't fit your bill. Mentoring is a two-way street.

→ *Take time to find your mentors.*

While you may identify ideal mentors quickly, you may have to invest a great deal of time in sincere introspection—and dedicated searching—to find just the right people. It will help if you create a profile of your ideal mentors before beginning your search. Consider age, experience, proximity, gender, reputation, availability, and credibility.

→ *Set ground rules with your mentors governing your interactions.*

Your mentors should clearly understand what you see as your obligations and contributions. By putting this in writing, you'll have a document you can refer to at your first meeting. Be sure to include how you will cover expenses, as well as when, where, and how to contact your mentor. "I'll never call you before eight in the morning or after nine at night," or "I won't bother you on weekends." Don't expect to assign tasks to your mentor.

→ *Honor and respect your mentors in word and deed.*

Thank, or repay, your mentors in some small way. Sometimes writing a letter describing the impact your mentor is making in your life is a nice way to give a sincere thank-you. Always speak highly of your mentor to others, and when something goes right, give the mentor credit.

→ *Don't argue with your mentors.*

Your mentors should not have to sell you on their ideas and suggestions. If you argue with their ideas, express your concern or doubt as a question, such as, "I must not be getting something. Why do you think that would work in my situation?"

→ *Provide your mentors with positive feedback.*

Let mentors know when ideas they proposed work, and how well, and when possible, quantify your result. "As a result of your suggestion, I sold ten more new cars last month, and now I am the top salesperson." Don't report on a mentor's ideas that didn't work out so well, unless you are specifically asked to do so.

➡ *Provide your mentors with all the truthful information they need to make wise suggestions.*

You must level with mentors, because they can't help you if you are holding back information or only share half-truths with them. Ask mentors to tell you what they think you need to change or improve— even if it might hurt your feelings. Be specific when you would prefer the information you're providing to remain confidential.

➡ *Use your mentors wisely and sparingly.*

Don't ask your mentors to solve all your problems. Instead focus only on those within their area of expertise. Don't abuse a mentor's time or goodwill—the more successful a mentor, the more valuable is his or her time, so use it wisely. For instance, write down key questions you'd like to have answered before calling your mentor, and don't just pass the time of day unless your mentor signals he or she wants to do so.

➡ *Let your mentors know when their services are no longer needed.*

Let your mentors know when you are ready to move on. You'll rely on some mentors for a day, others for a year, and you'll want some mentors at your side for as long as you live. If you know a mentor's usefulness to you has come to an end, it's time to send the person a small gift and a letter, letting them know how much help they've given you and giving them a heartfelt thanks for their services, advice, and help.

➡ *Seek feedback and make corrections.*

Adjustments and change are necessary for achieving anything at high levels. Why is it that archery targets feature three or more concentric circles around the bull's-eye? The circles let the archers know how to make the necessary adjustments, so they'll hit the bull's-eye more often. So it is, too, with pursuing your Core Desires—check for feedback from time to time. A mentor will be the best source for course correction.

If you have identified your Core Desires, you can begin your search for mentors today and begin living the life you were meant to live. While books provide knowledge, wise individuals provide practical advice based on life experience.

> *"A single conversation across a table from a wise mentor is worth a month's study of books."*
>
> —Ancient proverb

PART 3

Application
Areas

Creating Great Family Relationships

No other success can compensate for failure in the home. — DAVID O. McKAY

When asked what is most important to them, most people respond with one word—family. When you have a family where love is expressed, and shown, the benefits are overwhelming. A happy family where respect, laughter, love, and fun exist is truly a bit of heaven on earth.

> "A family is but an earlier heaven."
> —Sir John Bowring

If your spouse is thoughtful, supportive, a teammate, and a friend, you'll attain greater happiness in all areas of life. If your children are close to you, bonding as siblings, developing mentally, physically, and spiritually, who can measure the joy you will know? When the trials of the world weigh heavily upon you, your family becomes a true source of strength, encouragement, and peace—a shelter from the storm.

How can you create a satisfactory family life and still have everything you want in other areas? Is it possible to have a great family life while still accomplishing much outside the home? Not only is it possible—*it must be done.* Many parents achieve this balance every day.

CORE DESIRES IN YOUR FAMILY

In all of areas of life, the driving force that causes anything to happen with a high degree of joy and satisfaction is a Core Desire. If your desire is there, it's assured that you can achieve a close family unit. The results you achieve will be directly proportional to what you want and what you do. How soon you achieve your desired results is also directly related to how much you want them. If you are committed to something 100 percent in your family relationships, you can achieve it—especially if you seek direction on how to make it happen.

To achieve satisfying family unity, you need to be very clear about your Core Desires regarding your relationships. Virtually everything you want in your family has to do with feelings. For example, you may want to feel closer to your spouse because this makes you *feel* accepted, appreciated, valuable, and loved.

Poetry in Stages

My wife loves poetry, and for years I did not. In the early years of our marriage she tried to share her love for poetry with me, but I told her I just wasn't interested. I was never very sensitive or considerate about it either. Later I came to learn that not only did I hurt her feelings, but by being so adamant in my distaste, I forced part of her to close down. Not being able to share something so important with me limited our relationship.

I couldn't envision acquiring a taste for poetry, let alone ever becoming enamored with it, as she was. This was a major obstacle I didn't know how to overcome. I began asking myself what my Core Desires were concerning my wife. I want to know all about her—to truly understand her heart. When I am able to give her what she needs and wants, we feel closer.

I could easily see that my Core Desire was never going to be poetry, but understanding her was already a 100 on my Core Desire Scale. Once I understood this, I began to want to know why poetry touched her so much. What was it about poetry that made her happy? When I asked her these questions, she lit up. I could see that I was bringing her a great deal of joy just by caring enough to ask.

This was the first stage of my poetry experience with my wife. After understanding the impact poetry could have on her, I was motivated to please her, in some way, in this matter. Since

> "I have learned to use the word impossible with the greatest caution."
>
> —Wernher von Braun

we go on dates every Friday night, I went to the bookstore and bought two books on poetry before our next date. I had now progressed to stage two.

I planned a picnic in a beautiful park. After we ate, I pulled out the two books and said, "I'd like to read some poetry to you."

Her eyes widened, her mouth dropped open, and she smiled and said, "Okay!"

I opened the first book and began to read the first poem. It was a short poem—only about eight lines long. I may not have read it very well, but Marci got a kick out of my efforts. When she told me she liked it, I asked her what she liked about it.

She began to explain what the words meant to her and how they made her feel. I was happy that I was able to bring her that kind of joy. Then she told me it was even more enjoyable because I brought it and read it to her. That was music to my ears. When we had finished reading both books, I felt like a million dollars for making her happy by doing something she really loved—and she told me she fell in love with me all over again! Later, I even tried to write a poem about my love for her. This was definitely stage three. The poem may have been poor, but she was so pleased that it didn't matter. I have since written her several poems.

If you had told me that one day I would not only read poetry but write it, I would have said impossible!

We should use the word *impossible* with caution, however, for our Conquering Force knows no such thing as failure. If it is a genuine Core Desire, anything is possible. My persistence was automatic once I defined my Core Desire—to bring joy to my wife.

THE BALANCING ACT

Family life is always in flux, and sometimes these changes can be subtle, or take place over time. It is easy to say that we all need to achieve balance in our lives, but it can be hard to do—especially when we think balance means spending equal time in each area of life. Mothers can't comprehend how to achieve balance with just one child, let alone three or four. Likewise, career people often feel that they are too busy to achieve balance—that their job controls too much of their time.

Once you know your Core Desires and understand what balance really is, you'll more readily attain it. A balanced life should be the kind of a life where you have achieved a high level of harmony and satisfaction in all areas—at the same time.

A person who seeks wealth at the expense of family relationships, health, or peace of mind is not only *not* living a balanced life but is being robbed of the great joy to be found in the areas being ignored. The reverse can also be true. People who are so focused on family that they can't—or won't—do what it takes to earn the money needed to support the lifestyle they want are living an unbalanced life. These are people who are so focused on other things that they end up ignoring the most important people in their lives—their families.

You cannot achieve balance by seeing life as a matter of set hours devoted to all areas. By trying to give equal time, you quickly run out of hours. When you do the math, you'll find you sleep about eight hours out of twenty-four. If you work, your job requires at least eight hours, leaving you just eight hours to focus on family, spiritual, and mental well-being. No wonder most of us try to cram so much into the weekends.

Achieving daily—or even weekly—balance is very difficult for most people. However, you can certainly achieve balance over a fifteen- to thirty-day time frame. It is not only possible, but also very rewarding and important. If, in that period of time, you find any of your Core Desires in any area of life unfulfilled, you give them the attention needed to fill that particular cup.

When you are hungry, you eat. When your heart aches or longs for fulfillment in any area, do something about it. Whenever you feel that something important in your life is missing, that's a signal you are over-looking one of your Core Desires.

Balance means that we are getting whatever we want in all areas of life. Living with a deficit for a prolonged period always results in unhappiness, discontent, depression, burnout, stress, and continually thinking the grass is greener on the other side of the fence.

Because your children grow up and become adults before you know it, you must make the transition with them—treating them appropriately by recognizing when your job of parenting is over and offering advice only upon request. As

> *You can achieve and maintain close family relationships if you are unselfish and caring. Successful family relationships involve frequent giving, but there must be balance here. No family member can always be just a giver without the relationship deteriorating.*

your own parents age, you may find yourself in reverse roles. So flexibility, giving, sharing, patience, and forgiveness are all keys to success in long-lasting, bountiful, and fulfilling family relationships.

BEING OPEN AND HONEST

If you can communicate with candor and honesty, you will find you can achieve an incredible closeness and unity with others, as well as enhanced communication from them in return. A *USA Today* article, "Keys to Keeping Your Mate," reported the results of a survey about what people considered most important to maintaining a good relationship with their partner:

Honesty	96%
Discuss feelings	95%
Being good friends	92%
Fidelity to mate	91%
Support, encouragement	88%
Keeping romance alive	78%
Good sexual relationship	68%

Sharing financial goals   65%
Sharing religious values   52%
Sharing career goals   42%

Notice that the most important values are honesty, being open about feelings, and being good friends.

One of the most serious problems in relationships is a lack of honest communication. Most of the time we fail to communicate about core issues openly and honestly. We err on the side of tact and diplomacy. Sometimes, in order to communicate effectively, you have to be candid—or even blunt. Since trust is the foundation of all close relationships, you can't sacrifice honesty just because you can't find a way to say whatever you have to say tactfully.

Sometimes you have to tell someone that they are behaving or doing something unacceptable—or that they have offended you in some way. Be open and honest, but show an increase of love and acceptance thereafter. This is especially appropriate in marriages and with children but also applies to your business associates, extended family, and everyone with whom you interact.

Effective communication involves more than one person expressing a viewpoint, a thought, or a feeling and another person receiving and acknowledging the message. This is really only half of effective communication. Communication should serve a greater purpose between people and create a satisfactory result or benefit.

"Reprove with sharpness, but then show an increase of love toward the person whom you have reproved; otherwise, he or she may esteem you to be an enemy."
—The Doctrine and Covenants 121:43 of the Church of Jesus Christ of Latter Day Saints

For example, think about the last argument you had with someone. You certainly understood what that person was saying—you probably knew they were angry and why—and surely you expressed your feelings. If you both walked away angry with no resolution, then it is likely that only partial communication occurred.

Usually an open discussion with your spouse or child leads to something good. You gain a better understanding of them or arrive at a better level of activity, action, or solution. Calling each other names, yelling, or giving someone the silent treatment isn't proper or effective communication. To be open and honest at all times creates trust. People will say that they always know where you stand on things and that you can be trusted to speak up. People will cut you a lot of slack with regard to feelings if they can tell that your comments are sincere, coming from the heart, and have their best interests in mind. Try saying, "I'm afraid that what I have to say will hurt your feelings, and I don't want to do that. Will you allow me to speak the truth?"

When you mix tact with honesty, you enhance your people skills. If you can conduct your relationship with your spouse, children, or anyone else in this manner, your relationships will be based on trust and appreciation.

Often the main problems in a marriage center around the selfishness of one or both of the people involved. To attain greater satisfaction in your family life, you must stop playing games, be willing to change, to be open and honest, to grow wiser, and to become better. You must always keep the other person's best interests at heart and have reasonable expectations about what can and cannot be accomplished given the circumstances. If something makes you angry, say so. It's not necessary to blow up, just state your problem, with the expectation—and trust—of finding a solution. It's normal to exhibit emotion when you state the problem—don't pretend everything is okay when it isn't. Learn to focus on the problem and put both minds to work on finding the solution.

You cannot solve problems within the family by ignoring them. When ignored, problems only grow. Be willing to both give and receive honest praise and honest feedback—both positive and negative—and let other family members know where they stand with you. Be honest and open at all times, and eliminate game-playing.

According to one divorce lawyer I know, the biggest reason couples split up is their inability to talk honestly, bare their souls, and treat each other as best friends. Often when couples are dating, they play games with one another—always trying to put their best foot forward—and talk mostly about superficial things in order to impress each other. After the wedding, these couples find it hard to talk, hard to lay out a week's plan—let alone a life's plan. They fail to anticipate that their interests and ideas will change with age. They talk right through each other—rather than to each other—on important matters. This lack of communication often brings on drinking, infidelity, and physical and mental abuse.

I know a successful single father of two children. Being without a mate hasn't stopped him from balancing a busy home life with serving as president of his own firm. His Core Desires are to make his family work and still be highly successful in each of life's areas. He said to me one day, "I leave the company at the office. When I am home, I turn my attention to my two girls. You have to be able to talk—and listen—to your kids. They have their own views and opinions, and it's important that you listen."

FAMILY MEMBER SELF-ASSESSMENT

Maybe you know you have certain shortcomings that are standing in the way of attaining better relationships with the ones you love. Perhaps this quiz can help bring them to the foreground and help you begin to understand what holds you back.

- → *Emotional Intelligence*
  Am I affectionate? Do I readily and frequently show my love?
  Do my family members consider me to be warm?
  Do I pout and shut down emotionally when I am hurt or angry?
  Do I stuff and hide my emotions?
  Do I express my emotions appropriately, both verbally and nonverbally?
- → *Controlling Behaviors*
  Am I too bossy?
  Am I quick to anger with family members?
  Am I demanding with family members?
  Am I controlling of my spouse and children? Do I want things my way only?
  Do I interfere in the lives of my adult children?

⇒ *Maintaining Relationships*
Am I quick to apologize when I'm wrong?
Am I accessible to family members?
Do I help members of my family with their problems?
Am I generous and sincere in giving compliments?
Do I have fun with my family members?
⇒ *Making Contributions*
Do I do my fair share around the house?
Do I help set—and uphold—family standards?
Do I try to set a good example at all times?
Can my family members depend on me? Am I there for them?
Do my contributions outside the family make them proud of me?

These questions cover a lot of ground. We can all be more patient, control our anger better, and change our negative or destructive patterns. We can participate in family activities with our loved ones and come up with fun new ideas for family outings and new traditions.

HUSBAND-WIFE RELATIONSHIPS

Spending time with each family member is important, but it's especially imperative with your spouse. Children may come into your lives and add to the relationship you already enjoy, but never ignore your mate. My wife has helped me become the kind of man I want to be. Without her I could not have been successful in a business, improved in character, or have the peace and harmony I now enjoy.

As a spouse, it is your responsibility to help your mate become all he or she can be. If you aren't encouraging your spouse to move in the direction he or she wants to, then you're robbing yourself of the pleasure of having a companion and friend who is continually growing and blossoming. The more your spouse blossoms—especially with your help and encouragement—the better your relationship and the happier you will become.

Marital bliss does not lie so much in how romantic it is—for that

> *"The supreme happiness of life is the conviction that we are loved."* —Victor Hugo

will ebb and flow—but rather in genuine, unending concern for each other's emotional well-being. If both spouses have a never-ending concern for the other's emotional well-being, their love will flourish. This is true selflessness.

If you want to build a dynamic, loving relationship with your spouse, it is imperative that you spend time together doing things that both of you enjoy. Building a relationship like this is like building a million-dollar home—it takes time and the right materials.

Think back to the time when you were dating. You could hardly stand to be apart. You looked forward to spending evenings and weekends together. You were anxious to get off work so you could be together—even if you didn't have the money to go out. Why should it be different now? If it is a Core Desire to build a close relationship, spend time together. If it is a Core Desire to create this type of relationship, you will make it happen.

The best and most successful relationships involve two people coming together as whole individuals—complete in their lives, yet striving to become more. As these two individuals come together, fall in love, and choose to spend the rest of their lives together, neither one needs the other for joy and happiness—they were happy with themselves to begin with—but as they unite, the two worlds that they bring together are increased. When these two people come together, they superimpose their lives upon one another, and they become more. Their worlds instantly become larger, with much more to explore and experience.

Real Intimacy

There was a time when my wife and I realized we were not as close as we would like to be. Life had become very hectic for us, with four little ones to keep us busy, and I allowed my business to take way too much of my time. After we acknowledged the situation, we decided to start dating again—doing something more than just having dinner and seeing a movie.

We decided to do the things we had done before we were married—we played board games, walked the malls, or just sat on the grass in the park talking and laughing. This brought the life back into our relationship that we had allowed to slip away.

You must devote quality time to any relationship, but don't just put in time, or it may become routine and empty. If it is a Core Desire for you to have a close, fun, intimate relationship with your spouse, you will want to learn all you can about relationships from a variety of sources.

Marci and I like to take classes and courses that will help enhance our relationship. Once, we found a seminar that was a must for us—although I didn't know it at the time. Marci had found an ad in the paper for an adult education course at a local university, and she brought it to my attention. When I saw it was a course on intimacy, I looked at Marci, kind of puzzled, and asked her, "Why do we need this?" The very idea that I had to ask was a clue that we needed it. Marci really wanted to take the course, but I was somewhat resistant because I thought I already knew what intimacy was.

Although I knew it was not my Core Desire to take a six-week course on intimacy—especially when I thought I already knew all about it—I recognized that it was my Core Desire to please my wife and make her happy, so I went to the class, unaware of benefits to come. The teacher was dynamic and knowledgeable, and I learned an amazing amount, including that my male perspective on intimacy differed greatly from the female perspective.

Once we both learned what intimacy really was—something much more than physical intimacy—our relationship soared to new heights. This seminar required only six hours over six weeks, but it changed our relationship forever. I never realized how much I didn't know. Initially I went to the course to support my wife and make her happy. I may even have gone grudgingly, expecting to be bored out of my mind. But when I arrived and started learning all the very interesting things that make up intimacy, I realized that until that moment, they were foreign concepts to me, and I was amazed.

I learned that there are three levels of intimacy: spiritual, emotional, and physical. I had them the other way around, thinking intimacy was strictly a physical activity. Boy, was I wrong. I was oblivious to the basic facts, and that kept me from experiencing true spiritual and emotional intimacy.

Each week we were given assignments and asked to practice lessons before the next class. One week it was the husbands' turn to do the assignment. Before giving the assignment, the instructor told the men that she had to tell us something very important—something that would be an eye-opener for us—getting us all on the edge of our chairs.

"Husbands, women like to be held. Just held. Period." That was it—the big eye-opener. Then she gave us our assignment. We were to pick a time during the week when there weren't any distractions; the children were to be in bed, the TV off. We were just to sit someplace and hold our wives. My response was one of confidence: "I can do that. That's certainly within the scope of my abilities."

On Saturday night after the kids were tucked in, I went and got Marci and told her I was ready to do my homework. I took her by the hand and led her into the living room, where we sat on the sofa. As I put my arm around her, she snuggled up to me. It was clear how much she enjoyed this, and I was proud of myself.

Approximately three or four minutes into this exercise, I needed some clarification. I am not a stupid man, but like most, I have been known to be a little dense in matters of a woman's heart. I quietly said, "Honey, I'm real clear that I am not going any further physically—I know I am not to kiss you or touch—just hold you. But can we talk?"

"No, just hold me," she said sweetly.

A few more minutes passed, and I was looking all around the room, biding my time. The television was right in front of us, and the remote control was within reach. I said, "Honey, I have another question. Can we watch television while I'm holding you?"

"No. Just hold me," she quickly replied.

It was obvious that my question was unwise because I definitely heard irritation in her voice. And this is where it all went wrong: when I raised my left arm and looked at my watch. This was not a good idea. She saw me, and it sent her a bad message. She became upset and immediately got up off the couch and stormed into the kitchen. I called after her saying, "What's the matter?"

"You wouldn't understand," she said.

"Marci, this isn't right! I was holding you . . . wasn't I?"

"Yes."

"Then what's your problem?" I thought I was right and that she was the one with the problem. I was simply wrong, and we never achieved intimacy that night. We both got hurt—and mad.

> "Wherever you go, go with all your heart."
> —Confucius

Over the next day or two, we got past this problem and never brought it up again. Three weeks later, I went away on a speaking tour for five days. I missed Marci terribly on that trip. When I arrived home, she dashed to meet me at the door and gave me a hug. I could only embrace her with my right arm, however, because I was carrying a heavy suitcase in my left hand. There we were, holding each other tightly. I was looking into her eyes—I had missed her so much when I was away and felt so much love for her in that instant that I felt tears well up in my eyes as I expressed my love and appreciation to her.

Then the light came on for me. I whispered, "This is intimacy, isn't it?"

Why was there intimacy at my homecoming and not on the couch? Once I understood the answer to this question, I knew what it takes to succeed in marriage and family relationships. My heart was missing that night on the couch—holding her was an assignment, and I was simply going through the motions. Going through the motions halfheartedly never brings true joy and satisfaction—let alone peak performance. When you go after things halfheartedly, you can easily become derailed. When you are wholehearted, failure is not an option.

True intimacy is the ability to talk and share on an emotional, physical, and spiritual level. Marci and I have learned simple ways to provide clear direction for one another to fill the emotional cup. One of the things we did was to write on the top of a piece of paper "I love it when you . . ." and make a short list of the things we love the other person to do for us.

We call this the road map to our hearts. Since most of us don't know what the other person wants or needs from us, it is nice to have a map that will take us directly to the center of the heart. This exercise eliminates the guesswork.

For example, Marci told me she loves it when I come home from work and seek her first, greeting her pleasantly and with a hug. This makes her feel that she is number one in my life. She wrote that she loves it when I come up behind her, put my arms around her and kiss her on the neck, and when I value her viewpoints and opinions. These are all simple things and I try to do them often, as it adds a great deal to our relationship. I laminated the list she made me, and I have carried it in my wallet for more than twenty years. I look at it to remind myself how special Marci is to me.

Love is a genuine concern for the growth and happiness of others. Your relationship with your spouse will grow dramatically when you share intimacy on all levels and bring mutual respect to your relationship. Simply saying, "I love you" won't melt anyone's heart if it is said without emotion. Try putting your arms around your partner and saying, "I'm sorry I made you think there are times when I don't love you. I do love you very much, and I'd hate to think of what my life would be like without you." You can feel the difference.

Paradise Found

Once, I went to the Grand Cayman Islands to speak at a two-week seminar. I was without my wife the first week, and so I never noticed the paradise that surrounded me. I called my wife and asked her to join me for the second week. The moment she stepped off the plane, Grand Cayman became paradise. The rest of the trip was glorious and fun-filled because I was sharing the beautiful place with the person I loved. I realized that paradise is not where you are, but whom you're with.

APOLOGIZING

A sincere and honest apology goes a long way to solve problems and patch hurt feelings. But an apology that carries with it even a hint of anger or unresolved feelings may as well not have been uttered at all. Saying, "I'm sorry, all right?" just doesn't cut it. If your heart isn't in it, it's not really an apology. An apology takes genuine feelings of regret and must be accompanied with conciliatory actions and statements.

For example, try saying, "Honey, I'm sorry I didn't call you tonight. I knew you were fixing dinner, but I just got sidetracked, and I blew it. What can I do to make it up to you? I promise I'll call next time. Will you forgive me?" See how much more that rings with sincerity? Your heart is in this kind of apology. (Note that often you can't come up with apologies like that without some thought and preparation.) You will be willing to apologize—even when it means swallowing your pride—if it is a Core Desire to be close to your spouse. If it is a Core Desire to be happy and maintain peace in your home, you will focus on what's right instead of who's right. You will apologize quickly, so the relationship can regain its intimacy. You will realize that it's "our problem" to solve, rather than pointing out fault. This attitude allows the two of you to come together as a team and solve any problem.

It is also important for children to hear their parents apologize, to each other and also to them, when they make mistakes. I once accused my two oldest children of breaking a lamp. They denied doing it, but I didn't listen to them. I was convinced they had done it. Within an hour of their leaving for school, I discovered that they hadn't broken it and I felt horrible. How could I make up for my false accusation? I decided to buy some flowers, go to their school, call them out of class, and apologize.

When I got to their school, it was recess time. I went to the playground and asked for a minute of their time. I got down on my knees and, with tears in my eyes, told them how wrong I had been—how ashamed I felt. I promised to trust them and asked them to forgive me, then I

> Parents make mistakes and should apologize when they do.

handed them the flowers. They threw their arms around me and told me that they forgave me and loved me.

My sons learned that their father sometimes makes mistakes, too, and that taking responsibility for your mistakes is the right thing to do. Apologizing is the honorable thing to do when you mess up, and love grows when this happens.

RESOLVING DISPUTES

In our family, we do not allow our children to fight with each other. We encourage them to express their feelings—they may be angry and hurt—but they cannot scream at one another, hit each other, or call each other names. Working it out is the only acceptable behavior. We frequently have to show them how to work it out, but this is how they learn.

In the long run, nothing is more important than marriage and family. There will be times in life when you must work extra hours to finish a project, travel, study, or prepare for a performance. During those times, your family will receive less time and attention. But rather than feel guilty about that, allow it to create a consciousness and a commitment to make it up.

Spending time with family makes good sense, and pays big dividends. What's more, it doesn't take a big income to enjoy yourself. Once, my wife and I asked a rather poor but very much in love couple how they were able to enjoy each other so much. They told us that they would put the children to bed and then they would have a date in their own kitchen. They would start with a candlelight dinner and end up playing board games. It sounded a little corny to start with, but we took their suggestion and found that if you play fun games you both like, you don't need to spend money.

Some couples think they shouldn't have disputes when their children are present. But how can children learn to settle their own disagreements if they have no model to follow? If children don't see you working out problems and difficulties, they may never learn what love is all about. Arguments between couples happen, but so does reconciliation. Children should know that we can work things out when we love each other.

> "The little world of childhood, with its familiar surroundings, is a model of the greater world. The more intensely the family has stamped its character upon the child, the more it will tend to feel and see its earlier miniature world again in the bigger world of adult life." —Carl Jung

PARENT-CHILDREN RELATIONSHIPS

For better or worse, we influence our children and help shape them. My wife and I have five children, and we try to spend time with each of them. Children learn a great deal from our example—far more than from our words—and so we try to be good examples in all areas of life, including problem-solving in relationships.

Seek and Apply Good Advice

In family relationships, seek input and counsel from many good sources—child psychologists, guidance counselors, successful parents, and religious leaders—and then weigh that input against your experience and ask yourself if it fits with the way you want to raise your children.

My wife and I once asked twenty-five other parents and friends who enjoy good family relationships specific questions about how they deal with anger, lack of money, and discipline. We asked about their mistakes in child-rearing and about what they would do differently if they had the chance to do it all over again. We found that people are usually happy to share their way of doing things. For instance, we asked the parents of nine children how they helped their children to sit quietly during church services. To us it seemed like a miracle. They shared two secrets: never feed them in church, and don't let their feet touch the floor. We took their suggestion and tried this with our children. We were pleasantly surprised when our children sat quietly in church. If it is truly a Core Desire to have a harmonious family life, you will apply the advice you gather from those who are already achieving the results you want in your family.

Once, a good friend of ours, Kathryn Kvols, stayed at our home for a few days. She is a recognized authority on child behavior and author of *Redirecting Children's Behavior*. At the time, the youngest of our children was just four years old. When we put our daughter to bed that night, she said her nightly prayer and asked God to "bless Kathryn and help her have a safe trip home." Kathryn commented on how incredible it was that a four-year-old would be so concerned with the people around her. Kathryn also told us that she had never spent so much time with a family of our size without seeing some misbehavior.

In our family, we express love for each other all the time. It's important to tell all your family members that you love them—frequently. You can't expect people to know what you're feeling, and they may not always know all the pressures or problems you face. By giving lots of kisses and hugs, they will know you think of them often and know how much you care. Even with older children, hugs are very important.

While I was speaking to a group on Padre Island, Texas, about creating self-esteem in children and the value of parents hugging their children all through their lives, a forty-five-year-old man told me a moving story. He said that when he was growing up his father never hugged him, and he now had three little boys that he didn't hug either. That day he understood the value and importance of showing his love to his family and vowed to begin hugging his boys. That was a wonderful payday for me, and the lives of his children will be changed forever.

POTENTIAL AREAS TO EXPLORE WITH FAMILY MENTORS

Children Ages One to Twelve

- ➡ Television: hours, programs, channels, and priorities
- ➡ Allowances: How much and how often? Discuss chores and restrictions.
- ➡ Computers: use, restrictions, ground rules, web sites, and computer games

➡ Room cleaning: frequency and what is expected
➡ Hygiene and health: bathing, brushing teeth, doctor and dentist visits
➡ Clothing: styles, designer labels, school clothes, and play clothes
➡ Friendships: selection, rules, overnight stays, and play at your house
➡ Activities, hobbies, games, and sports: participation, league play, and sportsmanship
➡ Homework: How much and how often? Discuss priorities, rules, and exceptions.
➡ Discipline: why, when, how, and what form
➡ Bedtimes: regular, vacation, summers, and any exceptions
➡ Music: what is acceptable and what isn't

Teenagers Ages Thirteen to Eighteen

Many of the topics for younger children also apply to teens.

➡ Dating privileges: frequency, age, date selection, destination, and curfews
➡ Use of family car: frequency, acceptable reasons, cost, and restrictions
➡ Part-time employment: type of work, hours required, and transportation to work
➡ Privacy: right to privacy, but need to know if they're exposed to alcohol and/or drugs

Adult Children Living Away from Home

➡ Car ownership: Is one needed? Who pays insurance and upkeep?
➡ College selection: Who makes the decision? Who pays for it?
➡ Credit cards: One or more? Why? In whose name will they be issued? Who pays? Discuss restrictions.
➡ College housing: Is it desirable or necessary financially? Any conditions?

➡ Summer housing: Is student to live at home? Pay rent? Why or why not? Establish curfews and other rules. Discuss room cleaning expectations and privacy issues.

Adult Children Still Living at Home

Many topics in the earlier checklists may also apply to this group.

➡ Support: Will you provide financial assistance? Why or why not?

➡ Rent: If earning money, should your child be paying rent? How much?

➡ Visits by the opposite sex: Will you allow the opposite sex to go into the bedroom? Establish house rules.

I suggest only offering advice to your adult children when it is requested. As your children become adults, you take on an honorary advisory role. Be more concerned about relationships than about giving advice or direction. Even with that in mind, there are always exceptions. You need to allow children of all ages to make mistakes, since they provide great learning experiences. However, there are limits. For instance, you have more home-buying experience than your children do, so when they're shopping for a home, you might want to volunteer your services to help prevent them from making a terrible and costly mistake.

When children reach adulthood, they want to try their wings and fly out on their own. There's a saying that when you let your children go, they return to you. They value the relationship and your friendship, and they stay in contact. When you try to hang on to them—or try to control them—they resent it and begin to reject you, and you run the risk of losing them forever.

Anyone who has ever attended college, or served in the military with new recruits, knows people who did wild and crazy things. Generally they are the ones who are experiencing complete freedom from their parents' domination for the first time—expressing all these pent-up feelings and desires for the first time.

Parenting is like teaching: The teachers who are the most demanding also earn the most respect. They come in, lay down the law, and take no nonsense. Once they establish that they're in charge, they can, and quite often do, back off on the rules and soften up a bit. It isn't long before the respect turns to love and admiration. The teachers who want to be popular with their students often let anything go in their classes. This results in the students losing respect for the teacher, and subsequently the students don't learn much either.

> God is the author of families. He knows that we don't know what we are doing. Mistakes are expected. Learn to be the best parent you can.

A study of children considered to be well adjusted and happy showed two surprising common denominators: a nurturing father and a strict mother. That is not to say that the father wasn't also stern when needed and the mother wasn't nurturing. They were both. Too many times, only the father is the disciplinarian and only the mother is the nurturer.

Children, of any age, don't always know what you are feeling. If you make it a habit to tell—and show—the ones you love how you feel about them, they will realize the depth of your love. Letting your children see expressions of love between you and your spouse gives children a sense of security that cannot be obtained in any other manner.

Put honest feelings into everything you do or say—whether expressing sorrow, trust, unhappiness, joy, anger, disgust, shame, disappointment, or unconditional love. When no emotions are evidenced, children and spouses can only guess. Be real with your feelings, so they can be real with theirs.

Once, I was wrestling with my five-year-old son, and my daughter, three years old at the time, kept saying to me, "Daddy, let me play with you, let me play too." She wanted to join in, but I rejected her request. I had planned to take care of her feelings later, but that wasn't good enough for her. She continued to ask if she could play until finally I gave in. I picked her up and tossed

> "One of the best gifts you can give to your children is to show them that you love their mother."
> —Spencer W. Kimball

her onto the couch, tickling her for a few brief seconds, making her laugh and giggle. Then I resumed chasing after my son, and we continued our roughhousing. Moments later, I saw my daughter standing next to us, looking hurt and ready to cry. Feeling guilty, I asked what was the matter.

"I want to play with you," she whimpered.

"I picked you up and threw you on the couch, didn't I?"

"Yes," she said quietly.

"And I tickled you and made you laugh, didn't I?"

"Yes."

"Then I was playing with you, wasn't I?"

"But Daddy, it didn't *feel* like you were playing with me." She was right, I was just going through the motions.

Another time, our five-year-old son took a pair of scissors and cut his shirt pocket, for the second time. My wife was upset, as she had really given him what-for the first time around and thought she had put an end to this behavior. "Why do you do that? Do you think it's funny or something?" she asked.

He smiled, as if in agreement, but I saw a flicker of fear in his expression. I could see he really was afraid, and maybe even ashamed.

I put my arm around him and asked him, "What are you feeling right now?"

He burst into tears and then told me he was scared. When I asked him why he had cut his shirt, he had no answer. He was probably just goofing around, but he learned to deal with real feelings, and he felt very bad.

Marci came to his side, put her arms around him, and asked sincerely what she could do to help. All our other children did the same, gathering around him and encouraging him never to do it again.

INSTILLING SELF-ESTEEM AND RESPECT

Self-esteem is learning proper respect for yourself and having a sense of your own worth. I once knew a young man who was into all sorts of rebellious things. He dressed in tattered, worn, and dirty clothing and didn't take care of himself at all. When I asked him what he wanted out of life, he said, "I just want to be happy, but I also want to be an influence on other people." He was only fifteen years old at the time.

One Saturday I took him to a clothing store. I asked the salesperson for help finding an outfit for my young friend—a dark blue suit and a pair of new shoes. I wanted him to look sharp—like the president of the United States. Next we stopped at a barbershop, where he had his hair cut. Then I asked him to come to church with me the next day. He told me he hadn't been to church since he was ten.

The next morning, he went with me—dressed in his new suit, tie, and shoes, sporting his new haircut—into church. I stood back and took in the scene—his parents were amazed and started to cry. Others saw him, but they didn't know at first who he was. When they finally recognized him, they gathered around him and told him how fabulous he looked and how glad they were to see him. Everyone hugged him and paid him sincere compliments.

This was an astounding, immediate, and life-changing experience for him. He didn't want to go home when the services concluded. He felt valued, proud, and important; he'd never felt that way before in his entire life. He felt so good, in fact, that he didn't take the suit off for three days.

F.E.R.D.A.C.C.

To instill self-esteem and self-respect in your children and in yourself, you must use the following elements: feelings, expectations, respect, discipline, attention, compliments, and consistency. By teaching your children the value and importance of feeling loved, you'll help them become well-adjusted and happy adults who place no limitations on themselves.

"Train up a child in the way he should go, and when he is old he will not depart from it."
—Proverbs 22:6

Feelings

Addressing and dealing with your children's feelings teaches them that their feelings are not only real to them but important to you as well. Take care of your child's feelings as you would have yours taken care of. By treating your children as little people with real feelings and showing them that their feelings matter to you, you'll watch them grow up with the self-assurance that they have great worth and are important. Being sensitive to their wishes, feelings, and concerns doesn't mean that you always give in to them or allow them to have their way.

Expectations

Children usually become what you expect them to be. If they understand what is expected of them, they will eventually learn to provide it. Children may occasionally seem to depart from our teachings, but if we have high expectations of them, they will evolve to become well adjusted, happy adults. Youngsters need to know what is expected of them, as well as what they can expect from life.

Children need parents to set limits and boundaries for them. When raising our five children, we taught them that when they are small, their boundaries are narrow because they don't yet know what they are doing. As they grow older and more mature, their boundaries will widen as they take positive actions and make wise decisions. If they act immature or in a way that is harmful, the boundaries will be constricted, and some decisions will be made for them. The more they behave as adults do, the more they will be treated as such. Our children soon learned that they were the ones who controlled the boundaries, not us. We want them to have as much freedom as they can emotionally handle.

Be sure the high expectations you have for your children are motivated by what is best for the child—and don't reflect only what you want.

Respect

As adults, we often expect respect from our children. But respect should be bestowed on them as well. Treat children as you would want to be treated, or as you would treat an adult friend. My wife and I hold regular family councils with our children to seek their input on many things, like where to go on vacations, what food to eat, where to eat out, movies to watch, and even how we should solve specific problems. We do this because we want to involve them in all decisions that concern them as well as to teach them that their viewpoint matters.

> Tell your children that their judgment is valued. You can do this by providing all the known facts about the matter at hand, asking for their opinion, and implementing their best ideas.

Discipline

Discipline involves training that helps to develop self-control and character. Many parents perceive discipline as punishing children for infractions of rules—they may even discipline by slapping or spanking. But discipline means more than just punishment; it also means being able to begin a project and stay with it until it is accomplished.

Children need a lot of loving correction and guidance. You should have specific rules in your home to help provide the right direction. Then you can say to your children, "You can do anything you want within these guidelines. But if you step outside these guidelines, there will be consequences."

You should also explain consequences to your children. You and your child can even decide upon them together, so the discipline is expected—and deserved. Don't make all the decisions for them, but set down rules and regulations with their input. Issuing threats never works as well as agreeing on consequences.

> "Foolishness is bound in the heart of a child; but the rod of correction shall drive it far from him."
> —Proverbs 22:15

Attention

It goes without saying that children need a lot of attention. A woman I know had a two-year-old toddler who was getting into everything. She worked full-time, and when she came home at the end of a long day, the child would scream and hang on to her, demanding her attention. "He is driving me crazy," she said to me. "I can't get anything done because he is so demanding."

"Does he do that with your husband or with his grandmother?" I asked her.

> Children want and need our attention from infancy to well into adulthood.

"No," she said.

"Just with you?"

"Yes."

I suggested that before the child began to scream and pull on her leg, she might pull up a chair and let him stand to watch her cook, or get him involved with whatever she was doing.

Studies have shown that babies who are held and cuddled grow faster and healthier than those who are not. When a baby isn't getting the attention it deserves, it often cries until someone picks it up.

Whenever possible and appropriate, involve your children in every aspect of your life. We hear a lot today about spending quality time—as opposed to quantity time. Because most families are so busy, they find they have limited time, patience, and energy, but there must be a happy medium between quality and quantity. If Dad spends two hours a day with his nose stuck in a paper while Junior plays on the floor, that's neither quantity nor quality time. At the opposite end of the scale, ten minutes per day of intense time spent with a young person isn't enough to be considered quality time either—let alone quantity time. It is important to find the balance and provide your children with the attention they need.

> "Went fishing with my son today—day wasted."
> —Charles Francis Adams

> "Went fishing with my father—the most wonderful day of my life."
> —his son, Brook Adams

Compliments and Consistency

Use compliments instead of criticism with your children. Try to be positive and always see the good side of people and situations, emphasizing the desirable traits of your children. Compliment who they are, not just what they do. If your children think that you are impressed with what they did, they will spend the rest of their lives always trying to measure up, perform, and be okay in your eyes. Help them distinguish between what they do wrong and who they are. If you must criticize, criticize the action—not the child—trying not to make the criticism personal.

Consistency is always key with children. Children whose parents are constantly changing the rules—lenient one day and strict the next—end up confused. Children need to be able to trust the boundaries you have set and trust that they are loved. If you say you will do something for them, or with them, you are obligated to do so. Finally, be consistent in your discipline.

Creating self-esteem in your children can only be accomplished if it is your Core Desire, and it must be if you want a truly happy and healthy family life. If you have a genuine Core Desire to do so, you will achieve harmony in your home. The ideal family life is one in which all are supportive of one another. This means that in spite of intermittent difficulties with sibling rivalry, selfishness, disagreements, and hurt feelings, every family member continually and unfailingly demonstrates—in word, in deed, and in heartfelt emotions—their respect and unconditional love for one another.

In times of difficulty, turn to your family and let them know you have a problem. Explain the situation, and seek their help with the resolution. I have approached my family many times for help with specific business problems. When I am unhappy, I ask them for support. There is tremendous teamwork to be found and utilized in that little nucleus called a family.

If you want to learn how to become a better parent, wife, or husband, seek the information from successful parents, books, mentors, tapes, and other sources. If your desires regarding your family are at 100 on your Core Desire Scale, you'll find that nothing brings more joy and happiness than a close family unit. It does take a lot of effort to create a pleasant, loving, supportive family—but it's worth it.

To better define your Core Desires regarding your family, take some time to respond thoughtfully and accurately to these questions. Don't limit yourself by restricting your responses to those that seem the most practical or likely. Pay close attention to how your answers *feel*. With each question, be sure to ask the Core Desire Search Question after each answer until you reach the core.

- ⇒ What would I do to improve my family relationships if I had more time?
- ⇒ What do I like—or enjoy—about a strong family relationship?
- ⇒ What do I really want from—and with—my spouse?
- ⇒ If I'm not married, do I want to be?
- ⇒ What were my desires for my family as a young unmarried adult?
- ⇒ What would I love to do for my family relationships?
- ⇒ How do I want my family relationships to improve?
- ⇒ What would I love to have—or do—with my family?
- ⇒ Do I want to be in this marriage? If so, under what circumstances?

Achieving Your
Financial Desires

The way to wealth, if you desire it, is as plain as the way to market. — BENJAMIN FRANKLIN

went from a low income to being in the top 0.5 percent in the nation in earnings in less than two years—and I only have a high school education. I am living proof that the lack of a formal education is not a hindrance to high income or happiness. I was driven by a Core Desire to make money because I hated being broke and I loved what money would give me. These are the real reasons people make money. Many different vehicles exist to make money, but it's your desire to make money that will drive you to success in that area.

Knowing that the power of the Conquering Force does not allow weaknesses or a lack of current ability to keep you from achieving and succeeding, you can face your financial fears and doubts.

First, let's get clear on what you must do—and become—to create the kind of income or financial freedom you want. It's more than just doing the right things or being involved in a good opportunity. You must have or acquire the right paradigm about yourself. When you acquire the proper self-paradigm, you will find that making money is not so hard if you desire it. Many say they want it, but they resist making the necessary changes.

If you truly have a Core Desire to improve your financial situation, you will achieve it. That is why there are so many rags-to-riches stories. People with little if any past success, experience, skills, money, education, or social connections have achieved incredible incomes, because they acquire critical paradigms of themselves.

When you combine three things—a Core Desire for more income, the Success Attitude, and a proper self-paradigm—your financial security is a foregone conclusion. You may get a new job at a much higher salary, get a promotion in your current employment, or start your own business. It's only a matter of time before the results will be there.

But you should realize that your Core Desires regarding money are usually not the money itself, or the things that money can buy. Rather, they always have to do with the feelings you have when you aren't living from paycheck to paycheck. You must be honest about your Core Desires and recognize them for what they are. For example, many people want to own and drive a Mercedes, not only because it is one of the safest cars on the road but also because it projects an image that enhances the ego.

Thoughts about money dominate our culture, and they can be either pleasant or disturbing. Most of the daily news today directly concerns money matters. Scan the headlines for yourself. I call this "hard money news." Although you are exposed daily to such items, you may be unaware of how often money is in your thoughts.

It seems that love and money make the world go 'round. Our fascination with money goes far back in time.

Money can be the root of evil or the seed of much good. You need money to support and feed yourself, to get a college education, to help others, to donate to churches and charities, and to raise children. It takes money to be a philanthropist and leave an endowment to support something you believe in.

Money cannot make you happy, but it can rid you of many things that make you unhappy. To make a lot of money and to prosper are not selfish acts. It is an intelligent and caring person's responsibility to use his or her Conquering Force to achieve prosperity.

Money will always be an important part of your life, whether you like it or not. Money determines, in most instances, the quality of your life. You can suffer the miseries of financial problems, or you can use your Conquering Force to solve those problems.

According to *U.S. News & World Report,* today's typical middle-class family actually has *less* money to spend now than it did more than a decade ago. Most people suffer from some conditions that hurt their capacity to accumulate wealth. About 95 percent of retired people are financially dependent; most are dependent on family, friends, or charity and find they must continue working—whether they like it or not.

> *"I know of no country where the love of money has taken stronger hold on the affections of men and where a profounder contempt is expressed for the theory of the permanent equality of property."*
> —Alexis de Tocqueville

Far too many people live from day to day, from paycheck to paycheck. They are just surviving, without the joy that can come from adequate prosperity. Most adults consider money problems their biggest cause of stress. The constant worry about money is debilitating. Worrying provides no known benefit and cannot change what will happen tomorrow—but it can weaken your faith, cripple your actions, destroy your peace of mind, and make you feel powerless.

Money issues are a major reason for the breakup of marriages. Money problems affect us all at one time or another, and many of us all the time. Since money problems can ruin our health, cause distress in our personal relationships and our careers, and destroy our happiness and our lifestyles, financial fitness should be a Core Desire for everyone.

Everyone with a Core Desire for financial fitness can achieve it. Financial fitness means being content with your financial life, not wanting for anything, and being free of pressing financial problems. If financial problems are inflicting distress or harm on you or your family, you are not financially fit.

Suppose that I have a crystal ball and can accurately foretell your financial future. You come to me and tell me you want to earn a hun-

> *"Money alone sets all the world in motion."*
> —Publilius Syrus

dred thousand dollars a year, a sixty-thousand-dollar increase over your current salary. Your Core Desire is to be financially independent, free of debt, own your home outright, and come and go as you please.

I look into my crystal ball and say, "You'll have exactly what you want. Your income will be a hundred thousand a year, and you'll be doing what you love to do. But it will take you thirty-nine months to accomplish this. In the meantime, you'll have many rough experiences. You'll start two different businesses, and they'll both fail. You'll invest fifty-six thousand dollars of borrowed money, and you'll lose it. You will almost lose your home and your spouse to divorce because you will fight constantly about money. You will struggle to provide the basics, like food and shelter, for your family. Your self-esteem will suffer, but you won't give up.

"During the course of those failures and struggles, you will meet the right people, who will teach you things you need to know. This will provide the impetus for you to go into a third business. Your third business will struggle before it begins making money. However, after six months your income will exceed five thousand dollars a month. From there, your business will grow faster than you can imagine. After three years you will be earning over a hundred thousand a year, you won't fight with your mate over money, and you and she will be closer than ever."

If you knew this prediction was accurate, would you start now? Even knowing that you would face failure twice in the first two years? Even knowing you would have family problems and financial worries? You would probably say, "I want to get started right away."

THE SAFEST ECONOMIC BET

To attain optimum fiscal fitness and balance, you will need to:

➡ Clearly define your financial Core Desires.

Ask the Core Desire Search Questions, and pay close attention to what is revealed. You will be surprised by your real motivation for more money. Remember that you're only interested in Core Desires—not what you think would be "nice to have."

Does being financially fit mean having more money? To most people the answer is yes. How much more money? Do you want to be financially independent or just free from financial worry?

➡ Define the self-image and characteristics you must have to achieve financial fitness.

Don't be discouraged if you don't think you have what it takes. Even if you lack the knowledge, experience, and contacts, don't worry; if you have the Core Desires, you can—and will—get the rest. The critical thing is the self-image and attitude you have. If you think that you must have a college degree to become financially well off, think again.

ACTIONS AND ATTITUDES OF FISCAL FITNESS

Henry Ford once asked one of his young automotive engineers, "What is your life ambition?"

The young man said, "I want to become very rich."

A couple of days later, Ford approached the engineer and instructed him to put on a pair of glasses, which instead of having glass lenses had silver dollars in the frame. Then he asked the engineer, "What do you see?"

Bill Gates, *one of the richest men in the world—a billionaire many times over—dropped out of college to pursue his dream. He was a billionaire by the time he was thirty-one, the youngest person ever to reach such heights.*

Bill Rosenberg *had to quit school at age fourteen to help feed his parents and siblings. He went on to found Dunkin' Donuts, and later sold it for millions of dollars.*

John D. MacArthur *had only a basic education. He became an insurance, banking, and land-owning baron worth more than a billion dollars twenty years ago, when accumulating that much money was much harder than it is today. His legacy to us all is the John D. and Catherine T. MacArthur Founda-*

tion, which provides annual stipends to creative individuals.

Ted Turner *was reportedly kicked out of college, but he went on to become a very rich man.*

Tom Monaghan, *the founder of Domino's Pizza, did graduate from high school— dead last. He never made it past his freshman year at college— and he tried several colleges!*

"Nothing," the guy replied.

Having made his point, the auto giant said, "Then maybe you should rethink that ambition of yours." The man had money right in front of his eyes, but he couldn't see it.

Making money is not just about doing things; it's about how you see yourself—and being the person it takes to earn it. If you want the flexibility to come and go as you please and the mobility to go anywhere you want, you must be financially fit.

Some people have jobs that demand a lot of time and travel. Others have the financial ability to go wherever they want, but they don't have the time. For example, physicians are frequently on call twenty-four hours a day. They carry beepers with them wherever they go. No matter where they are, they must respond—and usually end up dropping everything to attend to a patient. I have several physician friends, and because of their dedication and commitment, they cannot—or will not—leave their practice for any length of time because it would mean leaving their patients.

In one instance, both the husband and wife were respected medical doctors and practiced in different hospitals. Their professional lives were fabulous, but their personal relationships and family situation were in a shambles—there was no balance in their lives.

Another friend is chained to his business. He said to me one day, "I feel like I am on a runaway freight train—I can't get off. I don't have the time to do the things I really want to do, because this business is taking all my time." Because he is such an integral part of that business, he can't take time off.

There is a better way. You can avoid being trapped in a similar situation if you apply correct principles, both in the way you choose to earn more money and in becoming the person you need to be.

When it comes to making money, there is no limit to what you can do—if you truly want it with all your heart. At one time or another, I suspect we've all wondered where the money would come from. I've certainly been there before. But I also know that you can turn a bad situation around.

TEN TIPS FOR FISCAL FITNESS

Financial fitness may not mean being financially independent, but whatever it means to you, identify it clearly, and then you'll be willing to become what is needed.

To achieve maximum fiscal fitness, you must:

1. Want to make more money so badly that you will do whatever it takes—for as long as it takes—to make it happen. If you are compelled by Core Desires, you will have this attitude.
2. Love what you are doing. Many people only love part of what they do.
3. Believe in your product and service and know your field.
4. Believe that you are worth listening to. This instills confidence in others about you and what you are doing. You are worth listening to on the day you decide you are.
5. See yourself as a leader, someone worth following.
6. Find mentors to emulate—not only do what they do but be like them.
7. Be teachable. Learn whatever your mentors are willing to teach you, and don't be stubborn.
8. Believe that every problem has a solution, and no problem is big enough to stop you.
9. Get out of your comfort zone and take risks.
10. Acquire, and present, an air of confidence in yourself and whatever you do.

Don't let your financial past determine your financial future. You can learn anything you want; you can choose what you want to do and become and create the opportunity to earn as much money as your heart desires.

ON TAKING RISKS

One of the hardest things in life to do is take risks. Many people tell me they're not willing to sacrifice their security, and find risk-taking to be frightening. But once you realize that everything involves risk, your confidence becomes the cure for risk aversion. One survey showed that in order for people to succeed in business they need self-confidence, drive and energy, the ability to deal with uncertainty and confusion, and finally, persistence. These attributes will come naturally when you are doing what you truly want to do. When you are pursuing Core Desires, you are willing to acquire knowledge, skills, and experience, and you have the will to persist.

If your own self-confidence is low, borrow some from those who are confident. Follow their advice and become like them. If you wanted to learn how to swim but were afraid of water, you'd take lessons from a swimming instructor. You would borrow from their faith and confidence, do exactly what they said, and before long you'd be swimming. Still, at some point you would have to take the risk and get in the water without your instructor at your side.

It takes time to learn, but your confidence will be higher once you start down that path under the advice of a successful guide. So define your Core Desires clearly, and gain the motivation to invest time and effort to attain them. As you do so, your confidence will grow quickly.

Many people dart from one hot deal to the next, like moths to a flame, thinking each will be their golden opportunity but getting burned every time. Why? Because they don't change or become the kind of person it takes to make money from any business opportunity.

Many income opportunities exist, and many individuals who get involved make a great deal of money. And yet many more individuals get involved in the same opportunities and never achieve financial success. Although the company, the products, the training, and the commission structures are the same for everyone, only those who are truly dedicated to their Core Desires will ever have the success they seek.

> "There is no security on this earth. There is only opportunity."
>
> —General Douglas MacArthur

Success—or failure—in any opportunity is caused by something within the heart and mind of the individual. It is the Core Desire and a willingness to grow and become more.

> *A mentor's main role is to shorten your learning curve.*

When someone says they'll try, they are preparing to walk away from the situation later with their head held high, telling anyone who cares to listen, "I did my best." Core Desires eliminate "best shots." Persistence and determination play a big role in attaining your financial objectives. If you set out to achieve something with the determination created by a Core Desire, you will have the persistence to accomplish it.

Although I failed in several business ventures, I persisted. Don't say you don't have the time to do what needs doing in your financial area. Don't say you can't strain and stretch to achieve financial peace of mind. Just figure out whether you want it badly enough to do whatever it takes. If you want it enough, you will find you can handle things that you never thought possible.

> *"Do or do not. There is no try."*
> —Yoda, the Jedi Master
> in *Star Wars*

I know scary things can happen in the area of finance. Most successful people have had to struggle financially. Some have even had to file for bankruptcy. But because of their Core Desires, they never give up.

FLEXING YOUR FISCAL MUSCLE

➡ *Walt Disney* went bankrupt several times, yet he always bounced back—and created Disneyland in the process.

➡ *Steve L.* was the proud and profitable owner of a gold mine in another country. He was sitting on top of the world when the government nationalized his business, taking over his mine and providing no compensation. He lost it all overnight, and yet he picked up the pieces and started all over again.

➡ *David Butler* was raised on an Indian reservation. David's family lived on dirt floors well into his teens in spite of his father being a hard worker. They managed to get by but never seemed to get ahead.

By the time David was a senior in high school, he had decided that he didn't want to struggle the way his father had. He promised himself that he would never take a job to fulfill another man's dreams at the expense of his own. This was his intense Core Desire.

This innate desire caused David to have an I-will-overcome attitude. After years of striving, he became a distributor for a company that focused on health and personal care. Along the way, David had some heartbreaking disappointments and met with many obstacles—some of his own making—but he didn't quit. He learned what he had to do to change and forged ahead, driven by his Core Desire to be financially free. His Conquering Force was at full throttle the whole time, causing him to overcome mistakes and achieve a high level of income.

Today, with a six-figure annual passive income, David and his wife enjoy a life that is free from financial worries. He is free to be with his family, free to travel, and free to serve others.

There will be times, as David found, when you run into brick walls or dead ends, and you may become discouraged. Facing those problems and solving them may not be easy, but if it is a genuine Core Desire, your Conquering Force will assist you—and you won't quit until you have overcome the barriers. Some of the greatest adversities you face can turn out to be opportunities.

➡ *Kathleen Deoul* applied for a job at a large company and was turned down, but she persisted. One year and nine interviews later, her perseverance paid off when a company chose her as the first woman ever hired for a sales position on the East Coast. In spite of the daunting discrimination she endured, her relentless drive positioned her as the company's first major account representative. In her first year, she ranked in the top ten out of more than three hundred sales reps, breaking through several glass ceilings.

Having gone as high as she could go in that company, she left and started her own company. She became a leader in providing executive office suites for Department of Defense contractors, doing business with the Pentagon and the navy.

At the age of forty-two, while pregnant, she was stricken with a debilitating disease. She dealt with tremendous pain, an inability to sleep, chronic fatigue, and multiple life-threatening infections. Eventually, her ability to walk was impaired. She endured six major surgeries over a nine-year period, commuting 120 miles a day to work while enduring painful spasms in her back, neck, and shoulders. Things were tough, to say the least, but her Core Desire to succeed in business did not let her stop or give up.

While still operating her executive office suites company, she also became a distributor of health products for a company that had helped her with her physical problems. She parlayed this part-time business into a multimillion-dollar income. Over the course of just six years, she created a fantastic lifestyle. She says that her health problems helped fuel her success because she had to become knowledgeable about the health issues afflicting her. The very thing that forced her to sell her first business created vast wealth—and health—for her.

Kathleen credits her success to having a clear understanding of her Core Desires. She never practiced goal-setting, daily affirmations, or visualization. Her success is a direct result of her Core Desires unleashing her Conquering Force. With this power, she got past all the problems, disappointments, physical struggles, and discouragement.

➡ *Dave Johnson* was newly married when he found himself in a job he disliked. He decided to join the navy and take advantage of both their training and the GI Bill. He felt the navy would be a good way to begin an electronics career.

One day while working on some electronic equipment, he realized that this was not what he wanted to be doing for the next thirty years. He remembered the leader of his church telling him, "Happy is the man who has found his worship, wife, and work—and loves all three." Dave only had two of the three—he loved his worship and his wife. Now he needed to find work that he dearly loved.

At a business meeting, Dave heard an extremely successful man speak. After the lecture, the host told the speaker, "These people will never be the same because you came here today."

That statement had a deep impact on Dave, and he knew he had found what he was looking for. He, too, wanted to know that people would be changed for the better because of him. He had connected to a deep-rooted Core Desire. He immediately set out looking for a career where he could uplift people and realize his desire.

Dave was struggling to make ends meet. He lived in a modest house and could not afford to feed his nine children. He was "financially terminal," at rock bottom, and in great despair. At age forty he had expected to be rich and famous. Instead he was broke and embarrassed.

Dave began a home-based business as an independent distributor of health products of a large Japanese company, and this time things were very different. He was able to generate over two hundred thousand dollars in income in the first year. Now he has eleven children, is debt free, and enjoys an annual seven-figure income. More importantly, he spends his days achieving his Core Desires— teaching, training, and helping others. He is making a difference in lives all over the world, just as he always wanted to do.

Dave's problems and challenges paved the way for his financial success. His struggles and failures strengthened and taught him. With each misstep, he moved closer to what he really wanted. Once he was clear about his Core Desire, it unleashed his Conquering Force, and with that force he overcame huge obstacles.

Dave credits his success to a powerful and overwhelming desire to make a difference. He knows that obstacles may slow you down, but they cannot stop you.

No obstacle can keep you away from a 100 on your Core Desire Scale. If you truly want to have more income, you have the ability within you to create it. You must identify the risks involved with your venture, then move forward as if they don't exist. Be willing to fail— the average entrepreneur has 3.8 failures before finally achieving a success. True entrepreneurs never accept defeat. Failure bothers them, but they are driven by Core Desires so they keep going.

> *Don't say, "I am not the entrepreneur type." You can be whatever "type" you want to be. Not all entrepreneurs operate or act the same way.*

➡ *R. H. Macy* failed seven times before his New York department store became a success.

➡ *John Creasey*, the prolific English novelist, received more than seven hundred rejection slips before finding a publisher and going on to publish over five hundred books.

➡ *Thomas Edison*, one of the greatest inventors of all time, said, "If you aren't succeeding at the rate you want, increase your rate of failure."

We've all heard that it took him ten thousand failures before he got a light bulb to work. "At least I know ten thousand ways it won't work," he said.

There's an element of risk in almost every decision. Deciding not to take a risk could mean losing out on some of life's greatest joys and experiences.

WHAT ABOUT YOU?

Can you see yourself making ten million dollars? Even if you can't, maybe you can see yourself earning fifty thousand or a hundred thousand dollars more. Are earnings like this possible, or probable, in your line of work? You can create any amount of money you want, if it is really a Core Desire. Find one—or more—mentors to show you how to do it, follow their advice, and acquire their success attributes and characteristics.

> *"Money is the seed of money, and the first guinea is sometimes more difficult to acquire than the second million."*
> —Jean Jacques Rousseau

If you worry about money, you probably feel powerless to make more, but this just isn't true. All you need to do is change your attitude, see the light at the end of the tunnel, and excitedly begin working on your new solution. But if you believe that hard work alone will be the answer to improving your finances, then your paradigm may be keeping you from experiencing financial success.

I know many hardworking people who never seem to have enough money. My parents retired on about sixteen hundred dollars a month—and they were two of the hardest working people I know. Hard work alone isn't the answer—unless it is hard work applied properly in areas that can create wealth, combined with correct self-paradigms and a Core Desire to do so. Once you unleash your Conquering Force, you automatically have the enthusiasm to work toward any financial objective you identify, whether it is an additional five hundred dollars a month or a million dollars in net worth. It doesn't matter how you choose to make money. But you will have to do things differently and be something more than you are at this time. Money can't buy happiness, but it sure can help you get rid of many of the things that cause unhappiness.

> *"If money is your hope for independence you will never have it. The only real security that a man [or woman] will have in this world is a reserve of knowledge, experience, and ability."* —Henry Ford

9

Enhancing Your Self-Image

*Never esteem anything as an advantage to you
that will make you break your word or lose your
self-respect.* — MARCUS AURELIUS ANTONINUS

Success is an inside job. Even if your body and mind are ready, willing, and able to learn and do whatever is necessary to get the job done, a negative self-image may stop you.

Although we create many outward images of ourselves—so we can interact with or impress others and sell our ideas or services—we only have one self-image. The way we view ourselves determines the level of success we attain in anything. To achieve more success, some parts of our sense of self will have to change.

Your inward impression of yourself controls much of what you create in your life. When someone says, "Good morning, how are you?" you probably answer, "Fine," regardless of any troubles you may be having. The image you project is often very different from your true sense of self.

Because your level of success and happiness is controlled by your interior self-image, you must try to ensure that your exterior image and your interior image are in sync. If you can't match your self-worth with your exterior image, your ability to achieve at the highest levels will be restricted.

Try this exercise. Put the palms of your hands together with the fingers aligned as if in prayer. These hands pressing gently together represent you. Now twist your wrists, keeping your hands together, until the back of your right hand is facing away from your face. The right hand with its back facing out is the side of you that you want and allow the world to see. In fact, you present it to the world all the time. You put your best foot forward. It is the side of you that is happy, fine, capable, reliable, strong, honest, trustworthy, caring, sensitive, and thoughtful. This is your positive side.

Your left hand is the one only you can see. It's the side of you that isn't so good. This is the side of you that's not strong, that is lonely or hurting, that has faults, is afraid, unhappy, easily angered, and not confident. This is your not-so-positive side.

Which side is the real you—the positive side or the not-so-positive side? The truth is, you are both. One side does not negate the other. Just because you have faults, failures, or insecurities doesn't negate the fact that you have strengths, wonderful attributes, and abilities to get things done. Yet most people tend to let their not-so-positive side reduce the strengths on the positive side. They focus on the not-so-good side of themselves, saying, "I know I'm a good person, but. . . ."

If the image you have of yourself consists of only undistinguished and unexceptional qualities—or all the things you are not—then your self-image is discrediting your positive attributes. You can be—and in fact are—both at the same time. For example, if you get a pimple on your nose, isn't that all you see when you look in the mirror? Even though the rest of your face is just fine, you worry about the one blemish. But your pimple does not negate the wonderfulness of all your other features.

You can choose to put the not-so-positive side into proper perspective by no longer making it your focus. Once you have the right perspective, you are free to see all the good things about yourself. You can see that you have a profusion of strengths and abilities.

When people operate from the not-so-positive side, they give themselves negative labels, saying, "I don't really have what it takes," or "I'm not cut out for this." Often these labels are not true, but if they are your truth, a negative self-image results and affects your confidence, performance, and happiness.

To better understand how both sides are valuable to you, try another exercise. Put your hands in front of your chest, as if praying. Press them together as hard as you can, having someone hold your wrists at the same time. Now have them quickly pull your hands apart, moving one hand toward yourself and the other toward your partner. No matter how strong you are, or how hard you try, you will not be able to keep your hands together. Just as you are weak in trying to hold your hands together, you will be weakened if you consider your inner and outer selves as two separate beings.

Try this exercise again, this time interlocking your fingers. In this position, your hands cannot be pulled apart—you are strong now. As you can see, our weaknesses can actually make us stronger. Weaknesses tend to make us more humble and teachable. If you can believe that a weakness is truly a gift from God, then you must also believe that God will show you your weakness and make it your strength.

As a child, my weakness was my cowardice. That weakness prompted me to excel at karate. My lack of self-esteem as a young boy living on the Navajo reservation was one reason I decided to become a professional speaker and help others—so I could feel better about myself. My weaknesses have made me stronger.

If you are prone to take charge of a job and do it well, you are most likely driven by a weakness. This weakness could be a feeling of inferiority that makes you go out of your way to do well. Your feelings of inadequacy may cause you to be a top performer. In order to control the outcome, you have to take charge. Perhaps you have a need to be noticed, praised, or acknowledged that causes you to excel.

I know many people who appear to be very strong—they look and act like confident, make-it-happen, take-charge people. They get the job done, reach out to others, and are there to help whenever they can. Many are known for their caring hearts. But if they stop helping others, they feel empty and much of their joy goes away. On the surface, they seem fine, but inside they just aren't happy. For these people, helping others is like getting an emotional fix. They must help others to feel okay inside.

When I ask, "Who takes care of you?" I frequently hear, "No one."

Such people feel lonely and are either unaware of their need to be taken care of or try to ignore it and meet their needs by helping others. Often the reason they reach out to others is because they know how bad it feels not to be taken care of. Because of our weaknesses—or needs—we feel powerful or compassionate, but we can still be left searching for our own happiness. When we are just givers, our own emotional resources quickly become drained.

Oprah Winfrey

"One of my strongest memories is of being at a boxing match where Mike Tyson was fighting Tyrell Biggs. I remember hearing the announcer say, 'In this corner, wearing black trunks, and weighing 218 pounds, Mike Tyson.' He was exactly the same weight I was.

"I thought, 'I weigh as much as the heavyweight champion of the world.' I left there determined once again to do something about my weight. But it wasn't easy. During a four-year period, my goal was to get below 200 pounds. I tried every diet program imaginable and no matter what I did, I couldn't drop below 200. I would start a workout program and be inconsistent, fail, and gain more weight.

"In the weeks working with trainer Bob Greene, I started to lose weight. But Bob didn't want me to weigh in. He wanted me to be moving toward a healthier lifestyle and not measuring my life in terms of weight. I started to feel lighter and better about myself.

"All of the information about exercise, eating right, and how my body works helped me change the physical me. The most important part is to understand that it's not as much about the weight as it is about making the connection. That means looking after yourself every day and putting forth your best effort to love yourself enough to do what's best for you.

"The biggest change I've made is a spiritual one. It comes from the realization that taking care of my body and my health is one of the greatest kinds of love I can give myself. Every day I put forth the effort to take care of myself. Only when you have self-awareness can you achieve self-acceptance. Only when you accept yourself can you experience self-love. And when you are capable of self-love, you learn to love. To express love is our ultimate goal. This is the path that leads you to the connection. And making the connection will change your life."

Nathaniel Branden

"Self-esteem is the disposition to experience oneself as being competent to cope with the basic challenges of life and of being worthy of happiness. It is confidence in the efficacy of our mind, in our ability to think. By extension, it is confidence in our ability to learn, make appropriate choices and decisions, and respond effectively to change. It is also the experience that success, achievement, fulfillment, and happiness are right and natural for us. If you are mindful in this area, you see that self-esteem is not a free gift of nature. It has to be cultivated. It cannot be acquired by blowing oneself a kiss in the mirror and saying, 'Good morning, Perfect.' It cannot be attained by being showered with praise, or by sexual conquests, by material acquisitions, or by a hypnotist planting the thought that one is wonderful. Self-esteem can't be attained by allowing young people to believe they are better students than they really are; faking reality is not a path to mental health or authentic self-assurance. However, just as people dream of attaining effortless wealth, so they dream of attaining effortless self-esteem—and unfortunately, the marketplace is full of panderers to this longing. Self-esteem reflects our deepest vision of our competence and worth.

"Whether or not we admit it, there is a level at which all of us know that the issue of our self-esteem is of the most burning importance. Evidence for this observation is the defensiveness with which insecure people may respond when their errors are pointed out. Or the extraordinary feats of avoidance and self-deception people can exhibit with regard to gross acts of irresponsibility. Or the foolish and pathetic ways people sometimes try to prop up their egos by the wealth or prestige of their spouse, the make of their automobile, the fame of their dress designer, or the exclusiveness of their golf club."

You must drill down to the core of your heart to find the real truth about you as a person. The real truth is always much better than your truth about you. Generally, the way others see you is much better than the way you see yourself. Change your self-paradigm and accept the truth about yourself—that is how you will begin to grow and achieve differently. As your belief in yourself increases, so does your ability to accomplish anything your heart desires. Your life will become much richer.

ASK YOURSELF THIS

⇒ Does it matter how others perceive me?

⇒ Will their view of me affect my life?

⇒ Will the way others see me affect my income?

⇒ Will the way I am viewed by others affect my social life?

⇒ Will others' view of me affect my marriage and my children?

⇒ How does the way people perceive me affect my confidence and happiness?

How others perceive you and how you perceive yourself are critical to your success and achievement. How you act, talk, walk, dress, and present yourself have a direct affect on all aspects of your life. Self-image can have a major influence on such things as finding a spouse, earning an impressive income, getting involved with life, and getting the maximum out of it.

OUTWARD APPEARANCE

Your outward impression can also determine the level of your success. Studies by sociologists have tried to determine which is more significant—image or skill. They sent fifteen actors and fifteen skilled professionals to apply for the same job. The actors knew little or nothing about the duties required for the job—they just faked it. More often than not, the actor—not the qualified professionals—received the job offer. Actors are excellent at making good impressions. They know all about posture, body language, dressing for success, inflection in language, and facial expression.

When I ask people what they think it means to acquire a good self-image in the physical area of their lives, I usually hear "get in shape," "lose weight," or "lift weights." Occasionally I hear that they want to learn self-defense or buy new clothes.

Your physical image is very important, and it means much more than just getting into shape, losing weight, or doing exercises. It also involves appearance, clothing, color, posture, and style.

When I was just starting in business, I was struggling financially. I had learned about the significance of a proper appearance, and I always wore a nice suit when meeting a potential client. Once a potential client told me, "You're obviously successful, and that gives me a lot of comfort in doing business with you." When I asked her why she felt that way, she said, "Well, you look successful. You have a great office, you sound confident, so I assume that you are."

If your personal appearance is a turnoff, it will never matter if you have talent or ability. The way you package yourself has as much—or more—to do with your success as all your talents and gifts. People rarely bother to open an unattractive package, even if the contents are valuable. Because poor appearance is a turnoff, people are likely to seek a more attractive package and take their chances.

Your great ability can be obscured by your personal appearance; it may never be recognized—or tested—if your appearance is an indication of mediocrity and nonprofessionalism. Of course, ability and performance usually determine whether you keep a client or job, but appearance may well determine whether you win the client or job in the first place.

Thousands of people have a self-imposed handicap because they don't present a sharp personal appearance. It's true, you never get a second chance to make a first impression. An appropriate outward appearance can dramatically affect both you and those you come in contact with.

Do you know what the best hairstyle is for you? Do you wear too much makeup? How is your posture? Did you know that rounded shoulders are often seen as a sign of lack of self-esteem—sending the message that you are undisciplined, lazy, or don't care about yourself? Should you smile more? Could you eat or sleep better? How do you deal with pain? Do you chew your fingernails, swear, or have an addiction to TV, sex, caffeine, tobacco, alcohol, or drugs?

I once spoke to a woman about discovering her Core Desires. When we spoke of her self-image, she said she only had two desires: to lose fifteen pounds and to learn some self-defense. Since she didn't mention it, I thought I would bring up—as diplomatically as possible—the gap between her top front teeth. The gap was such a sensitive issue for her that she burst into tears. Repairing that space was a Core Desire that she had ignored for years because she didn't have the money to repair it. Once she identified how intense this Core Desire was, her Conquering Force kicked in, and within three months she had cosmetic dentistry. She no longer hid her beautiful smile with her hand, and it did wonders for her self-confidence in social situations.

If it is truly a Core Desire, you'll find a way. If there's anything about your physical self that you don't like, you can change it—or at least your attitude about it. Don't limit your thinking when it comes to discovering your Core Desires in the physical areas of your life. Would you like to learn to ski? Fly an airplane? Paint pictures? Play the piano? Sing songs? Do you want to relax more, play more, and reduce frustrations and stress? Stress can ruin your health and take away the energy you need to achieve your Core Desires. Learn how to laugh and have fun again.

Would you like to fall asleep easily and sleep more soundly? Do you need to get your body into shape through exercise? How are your diet and nutrition? If you tire easily, feel poorly, or don't have much energy, you can't accomplish the many things that you are required to do, let alone the things you really want to do.

Do you control your tongue? Are you courteous and considerate? How are your manners? Do you open doors for people, let cars go in front of yours, show deference to elders, and speak courteously to everyone no matter what their station in life? Do you use clean language? Do you say nice things to and about others?

REAL LIFE, REAL PEOPLE

Consider some examples of the Conquering Force in action.

> *"I not afraid of storms for I am learning how to sail my ship."*
> —Helen Keller

Helen Keller

When she was just nineteen months old, Helen Keller lost both her sight and hearing. Yet she went on to become a world-famous author and lecturer. She inspired millions by facing these overwhelming obstacles and overcoming them. Helen Keller's achievements prove that you can succeed at any level you choose, in spite of the obstacles you encounter. All you need is a Core Desire—and a mentor.

Thomas Edison

Edison once said that his deafness was his greatest blessing because it saved him the trouble of listening to negative comments, in which he had no interest. Being deaf added to his ability to concentrate his aims and purposes in a positive way.

Glenn Cunningham

When Glenn was seven, he was badly burned in a fire. His legs were so badly scarred that his doctors told him he would be crippled for life. But this Kansas farm boy was determined to run and play like the other boys. No obstacle was too great, no matter what pain he endured. He carried on—nothing would stop him. With his desire to be as active as his peers, he threw away his crutches even though he was only able to limp from place to place. From a hobbling gait he went to a full running stride. He went on to break the world record in the mile run, as well as win an Olympic medal. Against impossible odds and when all seemed lost, he fought long, hard, valiantly, and victoriously—eventually becoming one of the greatest American runners of all time.

Wilma Rudolph

Wilma weighed a mere 4½ pounds at birth. By age four, she'd already had polio, pneumonia, and scarlet fever, leaving her with a paralyzed leg. By six, she was walking with a leg brace. By nine, she was walking with the aid of an orthopedic brace. And by the time she was thirteen, she was playing on her school's basketball team. At sixteen, she won a bronze medal at the Melbourne Olympic Games. In 1960, in Rome, she won gold medals in the 100-meter, 200-meter, and 4 × 100-meter relay.

Michael Dowling

When he was fourteen, Michael fell from a wagon during a Michigan blizzard. He was knocked unconscious and couldn't alert his parents. By the time they realized he was gone and went back to find him, he was severely frostbitten. His right leg was amputated almost to the hip; his left leg was removed just above the knee, as well as his right arm and left hand.

Because Michael possessed a strong Core Desire to receive a full education, he addressed a group of businessmen, proposing that they pay for his education—providing he would pay them back. Michael eventually became the president of a large bank, married, and was the father of five children.

During World War I, the government asked Michael to visit wounded soldiers in London. While in London, he was asked to speak to a group of soldiers who had lost an arm, a leg, a hand, or an eye as they were being treated in a makeshift hospital in the lobby of a large hotel.

As Michael addressed these men from the balcony, many thought he was minimizing the seriousness of their wounds. He told them that there were no grounds for complaints and that everything would work out for them. He told them they could go on and have full lives. The wounded soldiers became angry with him and began to heckle him.

Michael then walked over to the grand staircase and started descending. As he did, he told them how fortunate they were. But the booing and hissing grew more intense. He sat down on one of the stairs and took off his right leg. The soldiers became less boisterous. Then he took off his left leg, and the booing stopped. By the time he had arrived in the lobby itself—scooting down one step at a time—he had taken off his right arm and slipped off his left hand—and there he sat, a mere stump of a man. Michael Dowling made a difference in the lives of those soldiers, as well as hundreds of others.

Evelyn Glennie

Evelyn Glennie is pounding out a rare and brilliant career as a percussion soloist, playing with some of the world's finest orchestras and symphonies—never mind that she is deaf.

W. Mitchell

Mr. Mitchell was in a freak motorcycle accident and was horribly burned. He lost all his fingers and most of his face. After many years, he recovered from the burns and led a very active life—even flying his own airplane. One winter day, he failed to de-ice the wings properly, and moments after taking off, his plane dropped about seventy-five feet to the ground—permanently damaging his spinal cord and leaving him a paraplegic. While in the hospital undergoing treatment and therapy, he met other paraplegic accident victims. They were all complaining bitterly about the things they could no longer do. When he had heard enough, he said, "You keep talking about all the things we can no longer do. But I see it like this. Before my accident, there were ten thousand things I could do, and now there are only one thousand. I'd rather focus on the thousand left."

Mr. Mitchell went on to become the mayor of his town—even running for congress. In spite of being confined to a wheelchair, he travels around the world teaching people how to deal with what life throws at you. He is billed as "the man who wouldn't be defeated."

As a result of his accident—and the things he has learned since then—he has become far more successful. He feels he has accomplished more in his life than he ever imagined.

Christopher Reeve

"Many people have asked me, 'How do you get through this?'

"I say, 'Well, I'm not having nearly as much fun as I used to have, there is a lot that I can't do, but how do I get through it? Because there was a platform that was built over twenty-eight years of being an actor, facing rejection, learning the discipline of giving your best eight times a week, having made that commitment for something that I wanted to do with my life.

"Because I had a platform, I saw that there was an opportunity to help push science and to conquer the frontier of inner space. It's an incredible moment of opportunity. I feel that if I hadn't built a base long ago, I couldn't deal with it. But along with my family and friends, the support of so many people around the world, I'm able to go forward in a way that I never would have thought possible. We all have this inner strength within us—there is nothing special about me. You also can do it if you rely on that solid foundation that you build. If you take the opportunities that come your way, as long as you have some component of giving back to the world, the flow and ebb of your life will work. There will be ups and downs, there will be times when things make sense and times when they don't, but you'll be out on an adventure that's a lot more exciting and meaningful than just doing what's expected of you by other people."

Why were these people with severe physical obstacles able to succeed where others—without any disabilities—never even tried? What attitude caused them to deal with these horrible illnesses or accidents, these seemingly insurmountable obstacles? What is this attitude? They all engaged their Conquering Force. In each of these lives, we see people discovering and working toward their Core Desires. These are people who enjoy life in spite of its challenges. They excel, regardless of the trials they go through. In spite of the difficulties they face, they are doing what they love to do.

NOW, WHAT ABOUT YOU?

If you had determination like these people, think of what you could accomplish. The only way you can get that kind of attitude is by identifying your Core Desires—the 100s on your Core Desire Scale—and allowing your Conquering Force to propel you toward outstanding results. There will still be things that you will have to do, or go through, that aren't fun or pleasant. Life sometimes throws us curve balls that we have to deal with—these are the "have-tos." Life becomes boring and difficult when you're only doing the things you have to do to get where you don't want to be.

If your Core Desire is to speak confidently in public, how do you acquire this ability? First, you've got to love what you are talking about, or at least have a great deal of interest in it. Knowledge is important, but it's not as critical. Another valuable way to exude a confident aura when speaking in public is to take your mind off your performance and put it on the gift in the message you are giving. If you believe in your message, have strong feelings about it, and are not focusing on how people might judge your performance, you will do just fine.

As a speaker, I had to learn not to get butterflies and worry about my performance. Knowing that my message would change lives and focusing on this gift helped me overcome my nerves. I learned to focus on what I was giving the audience, and the butterflies went away.

You deserve to look and feel good about yourself, wherever you are and whatever you are doing. If you're in front of one person, a large group, or even a mirror, it's the same. In job interviews, the interviewer wants to know what value you can bring to the company—not just if you can do the job. One study showed that 65 percent of interviewers make a hiring decision within the first fifteen minutes. The study also showed that 45 percent of the decision to hire is based on how well the interviewees present themselves, 35 percent is based on packaging, and just 10 percent is based on skill. That's 80 percent of the decision being based on presentation and packaging!

If you allow your negative self-image to dominate your life, it will affect all other areas of your life. If you don't have what you want in the self-image and physical areas of your life, you probably haven't identified your Core Desires. Because your inward and outward self-image will affect all other areas in your life, you will be a much happier, more fulfilled person when you have the proper self-paradigm. Your Core Desires will be realized much faster once you have a proper self-image working for you—not against you.

> "Order and simplification are the first steps toward the mastery of a subject—the actual enemy is the unknown."
>
> —Thomas Mann

Cultivating Social Relationships

If a man does not make new acquaintances as he advances through life, he will soon find himself left alone. A man . . . should keep his friendships in a constant repair. —SAMUEL JOHNSON

To achieve a high level of joy and happiness in life, we must be socially involved with people. This involves getting along well with others, having friends and companions, and offering help to those who need it. We are all part of a social environment, and our social environment provides us with many opportunities for fun, excitement, enjoyment, charity, and love. Indeed, one of the most rewarding things you can do is to reach out to others—to connect with others on a heartfelt level.

Involvement with others, however, can also bring pain. You can experience hurt feelings, anger, character attacks, job loss, sadness, and loneliness. But you can use your Conquering Force to maximize the rewards and minimize the frustrations and pain. Achieving success in the social area of your life is the art of learning to interact with others and care about them—and their needs—while they care for you—and your needs. When you have social success, you experience an inner peace and happiness. You gain an incredible sense of value, while discovering how rewarding it is to be a caring and giving person.

> *"If you want others to be happy, practice compassion; if you want to be happy, practice compassion."*
>
> —Dalai Lama

When I ask people what being social means to them, they often respond that it means getting together with friends more frequently or making new friends—often including attending parties and other fun-filled events. The more socially skilled people will also mention such things as being involved in the PTA or service organizations like the Lions Club or Rotary International. But there is more—much more.

Being meaningfully involved with other people provides a veritable banquet of wonderful heart-to-heart experiences. There was time when I didn't maximize the benefits that are out there to be enjoyed. The social area of my life has also become financially profitable for me—as it can be for you. In one instance, as a direct result of being involved socially, I brought in more than a million dollars to my company.

If you are not already a social individual, I encourage you to become one very quickly. You should enjoy and be enjoyed; love and be loved. Doing this is quite easy once you have the formula for social success, and it will help you enjoy greater success in other areas—ultimately influencing how much you earn, the services you receive or render, where you live, and with whom you work.

If you are seen as a great person to work with or be around, you tend to receive better service, earn more money, get promoted faster, and in general get along better. It is important that you learn the social skills that can make you this kind of person. It can be as easy as trying to improve the life experience of those who struggle by showing them a better way to be—by word and example. If they aren't receptive, move on.

Everyone knows people who are difficult to be around. They are negative, pessimistic, easily angered, or arrogant. They whine, complain, and blame. These are the people who are not open to change or growth. Because they are unwilling to progress emotionally or socially, they stay stuck and don't enjoy life.

FOUR SOCIAL SPHERES

To help you understand the different places where your social success lies, I have identified four areas of social importance.

Connecting with Others

Making connections with others is not only vital to your growth, it largely determines how much you can—and will—enjoy your life. If you don't have caring, giving relationships with others, not only are you being robbed of one of life's greatest pleasures, but you're also robbing others of the benefit and growth they would enjoy by interacting with you. At a minimum, you can find time to lend a listening ear or just be support-ive—you never know what kind of impact you can have in someone's life. None of us can ever calculate the impact we have on the world.

There is a story about a poor Scottish farmer named Fleming. One day as he was negotiating a narrow, rut-filled road that went past a muddy bog, he heard someone screaming for help. Dropping his load, he ran to the bog where he found a terrified boy waist deep in the mud and struggling to free himself. Fleming saved the lad from what could have been a slow death.

Days later, a fancy carriage pulled up to the Scotsman's humble abode. An elegantly dressed nobleman stepped out and introduced himself as the father of the boy Fleming had saved. "I want to repay you," said the nobleman. "You saved my son's life."

"No, I can't accept payment for what I did," said the farmer, wav-ing away the offer. At that moment Fleming's own son came to the door.

"Is that your son?" the nobleman asked.

"Yes," the farmer replied proudly.

"I'll make you a deal. Let me provide your son with the same edu-cation my son will have. If your boy is anything like you, he'll no doubt grow to be a man we can both be proud of."

Fleming could not resist that offer. His son attended the very best schools and in time graduated from St. Mary's Medical School in London, later becoming well known throughout the world as Sir Alexander Fleming—the man who discovered penicillin.

Years later the nobleman's son, the one saved from the bog, was stricken with pneumonia. Penicillin saved his life. The nobleman was Lord Randolf Churchill, his son, Sir Winston Churchill.

Never underestimate the worth of your caring attitude. The whole world could change because of your single action. Don't be so busy that you can't take time to reach out and connect with others. It's easy to get in the habit of staying home and watching TV, but it's disastrous to your social life—so get out and visit places where you can do what you enjoy. Go to libraries and bookstores, take an exercise class, or join a chess or gardening club. Get out there and share your skills, interests, experiences, hard-won knowledge, specialties, talents, and heart with others.

When you are feeling down, sad, or worried, try not to be alone. Call a friend and be open about needing someone to talk to or be with. This will help stop the downward emotional spiral. It takes a lot of trust for you to be that open and honest, but it is worth it. Loneliness can destroy your physical and mental health and happiness.

Love Relationships

As I help people discover and define their genuine Core Desires, I find that the area that stands out most is the longing for a personal love relationship.

You must determine if you are the kind of person you want to be. Can you attract the kind of person you want to be with? We usually have a great deal in common with those we are closest to. Think about the people you feel close to. You probably have similar beliefs, laugh at the same jokes, and share interests in movies, sports, styles, food, and hobbies. The more you have in common with a person, the more enjoyable the relationship will be and the faster it will grow and thrive.

In any relationship, there will always be some things that you won't have in common—that's to be expected and accepted. When I met my wife, I was very involved and passionate about karate. She wasn't. Instead, she loved musicals. I didn't. But we found that the things of most importance were the things we had in common. If you can share values and principles, ideas about how to raise children, religion—the things that really matter—then you can easily get past karate or musicals.

John Gray

"We all have many God-given gifts. The challenge with which we are each faced is to discover these gifts and then make full use of them by serving others. That is how our soul grows. But though our soul thrives when we give of ourselves, we must realize that we cannot give love unless we can receive love. Our ability to receive love is based upon our ability to feel, because it is through our feelings that we are able to receive support and then be motivated to give support. To give of ourselves, we must nurture ourselves. One of the ways we receive this nurturing is through having a good relationship. This gives us the opportunity to serve our partner—and serving others nurtures our own souls.

"Men and women receive love differently. The primary way to love a man and help him get in touch with his feelings is to appreciate him for what he does. You must repeatedly send him the message that he makes a difference, that his actions are worthwhile. You must also let him know that when his actions are mistakes, they are forgivable. You must assure him that he is accepted just the way he is. If you try to correct him or tell him what to do, he will only resist. And if he does not resist he will weaken; he will lose touch with the inner guidance that he needs to control his actions. Women often need to feel in control of their feelings. The way to nurture a woman's soul is to give her the support she needs to freely express herself, to talk about her feelings, her wants, and wishes. Don't try to correct her feelings or talk her out of her feelings. If she is feeling bad or afraid or angry, do not be critical of that.

"Once we have learned how to nurture our partners, we can then go out and make a difference in the world. Giving unconditional love nurtures us and fulfills our purpose in life. When you give of yourself without expecting anything in return, you become a bigger person."

In any highly successful relationship, you must be open and honest, as well as willing to look at—and own—your weaknesses and mistakes. Only then can you make the changes needed to allow the relationship to operate at the highest level possible.

When I was twenty-four years old, I was very much in love with a woman who hardly knew I existed. She was beautiful and successful, and I decided to create the opportunity for her to fall in love with and marry me. It was my genuine Core Desire at the time.

I began what I called "Project Pam." I researched all her likes and dislikes, I got inside information from some of her friends, and I received clear directions on how to be the kind of man she would want to have. I shaped myself into the type of man she should love. It was quite a project, and she ended up wearing my engagement ring.

Wedding invitations had been purchased, and we were to be married in a few weeks. Then disaster struck on a Friday: Pam called everything off. She said she just didn't feel right about going through with the marriage. I was devastated. The following Sunday, feeling angry and hurt, I asked God why this didn't work out. I thought Pam was everything I wanted. I was immediately overcome with the knowledge that there was someone better out there for me. I was overwhelmed by the intensity of that experience, and I trusted it completely. I no longer felt hurt, and I was over Pam. That same day I began looking for that someone. Within two weeks I met my wife, Marci.

I could have chosen to pine away, feel sorry for myself, and feel anger and bitterness toward Pam. But I chose to become excited at the prospect of finding someone else.

Marci and I were very sincere with one another from the start. We didn't just chitchat about our high school experiences; we talked about each other's attitudes, concerns, and desires for the future. That sincerity was vital in creating an enduring relationship.

In creating a loving relationship void of pretense and hypocrisy, you'll enjoy a great deal of harmony and satisfaction. I am grateful to Pam for

listening to her heart and calling off our wedding—I now know she was far wiser than I was.

Finding someone you can trust with all your
heart, who will help you become all that is in you to
become, is one of the most rewarding experiences
in life. The secret to a loving relationship is to be
dedicated to the concept of what's right, not who's

> *"The person who tries to live alone will not succeed as a human being."*
> —Pearl S. Buck

right, and to make a commitment to the person to whom you have given
your heart, making them feel that they are "number one" in your life.

True Friendships

Everyone wants, and needs, friends—especially close friends. You can
never say that you truly just want to be left alone, that you don't want
or need to have any close friends. It's a Core Desire for human beings
to interact with others—to like and be liked, to love and be loved.
Close friends permit you to open up and have fun. They like and
accept all the things that make you you—the good, the bad, and the
ugly. True friendship allows you to feel safe with another person, to be
accepted by others—in spite of the things you do wrong and in spite of
your idiosyncrasies.

Meaningful interaction with others is vital to your spiritual and
physical well-being. We can't choose whether we need—or want—true
friends, because we are simply not built that way. Few things in life are
more precious than the close friends who share your interests, pas-
sions, concerns, needs, hopes, and fears. Ideally, one of these close
friends becomes your mate for life.

When I was a child I had one friend, Teddy Begay, a Navajo boy. He
was my best friend, and he often defended me.
When I left the reservation, I didn't see Teddy
again until many years later.

When I was forty, I reconnected with him,
and we hit it off as if no time had passed at all. We
talked about becoming blood brothers, an old
Indian tradition. I asked him if the Navajos still

> *"One blessing of friends is that you can afford to be stupid with them."*
> —Ralph Waldo Emerson

did such things. Teddy checked with an old medicine man he knew and reported back that the ceremony hadn't been done in over a hundred years. The medicine man had never performed the ceremony but had been taught how many years earlier. Teddy and I asked the medicine man to perform the ceremony for us.

The ceremony was held in a hogan, a large mud hut with a door opening to the east, dirt floors, and a hole in the ceiling for smoke from the open fire to escape. Navajos came from miles around to participate because they wanted to see this unusual ceremony. The hogan was filled to capacity, with about twenty people sitting on sheepskins around its perimeter. The ceremony was done in the Navajo language, so Teddy translated for me. The medicine man built a fire in the center of the hogan and then chanted, prayed, counseled us, drew pictures in the dirt floor, and gave us things to eat and drink. In his prayer, he asked the Great Spirit to forgive him because he could not remember all of the ceremony, asking for it to be accepted. At one point the medicine man wept, and said that he'd never seen such love shown between a *bilagona* and a Navajo. At specific ceremonial intervals, each person in the hogan was given a chance to speak. Several guests apologized for the way I had been treated as a young boy.

The ceremony was a wonderful experience, lasting about thirteen hours without a stop. Teddy and I laughed when we wondered how long it would have taken had the medicine man remembered the entire ceremony.

I came away from this experience with a deep, abiding love for my new blood brother, as well as for the Navajo nation, particularly those in attendance. Teddy's mother, who speaks no English, is now my mother, too. After the ceremony I gave my new Navajo mother a hug and she hugged me back, which was unusual since Navajos of her generation didn't show affection by hugging. She smiled and called me *shiyazhi* (shi-yaw-zhee), "my son," and I called her *shima* (shih-MAH), my mother. I was given a special shawl, allowing me entrance to Navajo ceremonies or meetings.

The more friendships you have, the more open interactions you will have with others, and the more your life will come together. Your family life will improve, your self-image will be enhanced, and you'll enjoy doing what it takes when you're with friends. With true friends, you can be yourself.

> "What is a friend? A single soul in two bodies." —Aristotle

With close friends, you interact at a heartfelt level. When it comes to your friends, their feelings and needs are just as important to you as yours are to them. They care and worry about you, and you do the same for them. As you treat others this way, you experience profound happiness and contentment. With friends at your side, you never have to face the world alone.

To create closeness and intimacy with other people—male or female, young or old, family or friends—apply the following three rules in any circumstance.

1. *Be willing to trust that others will not hurt you.*

You must take the risk of being let down, ignored, manipulated, judged, or hurt. Even if it is risky, share your real feelings. The closer you are with someone, the more of you they can see. When you are close to someone's heart, or they to yours, you can see each other's concerns more easily. This can be risky when you don't know what they will do with what they see. That is where trust comes in.

Maybe you think that to depend on friends is a sign of weakness, but that's not true. By refusing to open up and share, you may be considered unapproachable or unfriendly—keeping you isolated with your feelings because you can't, or won't, let others into your life. People may know about your accomplishments and your possessions, but do they know about you?

How can we bear one another's burdens if we don't know what they are? Often we hold back from sharing ourselves because we don't want to impose, to feel weak or needy, or we don't trust that anything will change. Many people would like to have someone to help them and care about them but are afraid they will no longer be accepted or liked if they reveal their soul. The fear of risk shuts them down or closes them up, leaving their feelings locked inside.

What we often fail to realize is that the people who get to see all of you, love and admire you all the more. They empathize; they want to reach out to you and reassure you that you are liked or loved even more than before. So open your heart, even at the risk of getting hurt. The world is full of wonderful people just trying to make a happy life for themselves and their families. Most people have something positive to offer you, even if it is just a smile or a nod of understanding. Don't keep your heart hidden—it is far more rewarding to be open and vulnerable. You wouldn't stop cooking and enjoying food because of the very small chance that you might get burned, would you?

When someone shares something with you that is important, painful, or precious to them, try not to outdo them with your experiences. Rather, stay in the moment with their feelings, and respect them for taking the risk of sharing with you, creating a trust—the foundation on which all relationships are built.

2. *Stop playing games.*

Young men and women often wear masks and play social games because they don't know how to be open and honest—or they choose not to be. Men, for example, might exaggerate their incomes, plan "chance" meetings with women, and say the craziest things to try to get women to like them, instead of just being real.

Just be yourself. Don't feel that you have to put your best foot forward all the time. If you would like to meet someone, let him or her know. If you would like them not to call you again, say so. If something offends you, speak up. If your feelings have been hurt, be open about it. Don't pretend that things are all right when they aren't. Playing games only creates an environment of distrust, suspicion, and doubt. It is a far better use of your time to be honest, upfront, and sincere.

3. *Be open and honest at all times, using tact and diplomacy whenever possible.*

If you have to choose between hiding your feelings and being totally open, honest, and candid, always choose the latter. When you stuff your feelings, you only hurt yourself and others. When you guess about what other people are thinking, you're going to assume the worst most of the time—but you'll also be wrong most of the time. Rather than guess, ask.

If you'll do these three things in all your relationships, you'll succeed at high levels. You also need to encourage others to do the same with you in order to create an environment where people can feel safe with you. Don't make them guess what you are feeling. By allowing yourself to be true, you'll allow others to be open, honest, and safe with you, and then they can stop playing games around you.

Many years ago, one of my mentors taught me that sometimes the most painful messages are also the most beneficial. He was about twenty years my senior and also a very wise man. One day I did something unacceptable to him, and he gave me some feedback. He reached over, put his hand on my forearm, and said, "I'm going to tell you something that will hurt your feelings, but I'm going to do it because I love you, and I think you need to hear it. Is that okay with you?"

I said, "Go ahead."

What he told me did hurt my feelings, but I needed to be told. I was embarrassed, but he made me feel that I was okay anyway. I knew he cared about me and was teaching me by being open and honest.

Being open and honest can be risky, but it's worth it. If your intent is to help, not to hurt others, then make that clear to them. Most of the time people won't take offense, especially if you get their permission first, as my mentor did with me.

Where can you find people to befriend? Start looking in your home, neighborhood, and place of work—the places where you spend most of your time. You can create fulfilling social situations by involving yourself in your church, taking people out to lunch, playing golf, or going to a movie. You can go to concerts, the theater, auto races, seminars, flea markets, auctions, museums, and sporting events. The list is endless, limited only by your tastes and interests. To make new friends, you must create situations in which you're going to visit and share feelings, life stories, and opinions with them.

Social Caring

> "If you can't feed one hundred people, then feed one."
>
> —Mother Teresa

By reaching out to others, helping, caring, and giving of yourself freely without any thought of personal gain, you will become a better and much happier person—and your impact will be felt forever. Like the ripple made when you cast a stone into water, the ripple effect you create by helping others is immeasurable. If you don't know how to do this on a large scale, do it on a small one.

I know a man who is a full-time truant officer for a small town north of Denver, and also a member of an Optimist Club. As a truant officer, he found that some children failed to attend school because they were trading days with their siblings—there was only one pair of shoes among them. Because he was touched so deeply, he decided to do something about it and began a fund-raising drive to buy shoes for these youngsters. When he died, he left five thousand dollars to the Optimist Club, with instructions to invest it in a secure place and use the interest to continue buying shoes for needy children. Because of the lives this man has changed—and the many more he will continue to change—his memory will live in perpetuity.

One of the most rewarding social practices is letting others be valuable by giving to you. This can be very hard for many people. There are people who give and give, helping others do what they want or need to accomplish, but they won't allow others to help them. Some people will listen to your troubles but never share theirs. In most cases, the reason for this behavior is either pride or distrust. Giving is a good thing for everyone to do, and for every giver there has to be a receiver. If you won't allow others to give to you, you stop the process. Don't let pride or mistrust rob somebody of the privilege, growth, and pleasure of being there for you.

If you have a hard time receiving from others, or letting them see your deepest feelings, it's often because you have a Core Desire that makes you unwilling to appear weak or needy. Feeling this way may be so hard for you that you'll go to great lengths to avoid it. Your Core Desire may be to avoid, rather than get or achieve certain things.

Still, there is always a way you can reach out to others and show your concern for them on a larger scale. You can join local or national organizations or volunteer in your local school system. However you choose to give of your time, make sure it is a Core Desire. Keep looking for the 100s on your Core Desire Scale.

I know an eighty-eight-year-old woman who goes to a nursing home to help "the old people." She once told me, "I know I shouldn't call them 'old people,' but they are old, and they need my help." Her attitude keeps her from letting her own age and infirmities stop her.

People may not remember exactly what you said, but they will always remember how you treated them. Achieving your Core Desires becomes easier when you create solid, long-lasting, and mutually beneficial relationships.

> *"The friendship that can cease has never been real."*
> —Saint Jerome

Improving Your Mind

The renown which riches or beauty confer is fleeting and frail; mental excellence is a splendid and lasting possession. — GAIUS SALLUSTIUS CRISPUS

Everything we are, will be, have, or are yet to have is a direct consequence of what we learn and apply. Learning and acting upon our knowledge enable us to make meaningful contributions.

The more you know, the more you realize how much you don't know. You must continue to seek out new perspectives and truths to enhance your ability to achieve your Core Desires. Continual learning is critical and affects every area of your life. Learning is a lifelong process and should be fun and exciting, bringing you increased levels of success and enjoyment.

> "Nothing is more terrifying than ignorance in action."
>
> —Goethe

AN INVESTMENT IN YOURSELF

Learning is an investment in yourself. If you make wise investments in things that go to your heart, you'll receive fabulous dividends. If you invest in the wrong information, the data begins to collect dust in the memory banks of your mind.

> "An investment in knowledge always pays the best interest."
> —Benjamin Franklin

If you have any problems in your life—be they financial, marital, or parental—you will have to learn new ways to solve them. Most problems are created by the choices you made with the knowledge—or lack of knowledge—you had at the time. If things are to be different, you will have to seek new learning opportunities and fresh wisdom. If you don't learn more, you will stay stuck at the same level of happiness, income, and wisdom.

I know men who refuse to seek marriage counseling when their marriages are falling apart and they're very unhappy. They think that they are in the right, even when the evidence overwhelmingly suggests that they need to make adjustments. This kind of thinking is extremely limiting. This hardheadedness—and hard-heartedness—results when people would rather have unhappy marriages than face the errors of their ways. Their Core Desire is to protect fragile egos and low self-images.

Many people choose to be foolish and learn instead from hard experience. It is said that knowledge is power. Knowledge is not power. The proper use of knowledge is power, and wisdom. If wisdom is a Core Desire, you'll be more than willing to learn and apply what you learn. A little wisdom begets more wisdom.

YOUR CORE DESIRE FOR LEARNING

With so much to learn, it can be difficult to know where to begin. Focus on your Core Desires as a way of defining the direction of your learning. This will allow you to maintain peak interest while collecting information and processing data. If you are learning about things you are not interested in, your enthusiasm will quickly wane.

> "Knowledge is merely the expansion of our sphere of ignorance."
> —Albert Einstein

Suppose you have a Core Desire to learn how to ski. Eagerly you seek to accomplish this desire—you buy the best equipment, take ski lessons, and willingly stand in line in the cold. You spend time listening to other skiers reveal the finer points of the sport. You ride the ski lifts even if you are afraid of heights. Because you have this Core Desire, you go all out.

When you only think you might like to learn about something or feel that you're obligated or assigned to learn, you won't spend as much time or effort. You'll do just enough to get by. And at the first sign of difficulty, you'll probably throw in the towel.

Many individuals willingly take several "have-to" courses in their pursuit of their Core Desires. My daughter wanted a degree in Information Systems and Technology and took many courses required to earn her degree. She excelled in her career, landing a high-paying position at a major company. Although she may have disliked some of the required courses, she kept at it. They were the "have-tos" to achieve her Core Desire. As a result of the career she now enjoys, I estimate that these "have-to" courses were worth many times the cost of her whole education. Because she had the discipline as a result of her Core Desire, the "have-tos" became acceptable, as long as they helped her achieve her dream.

Formal education isn't the only way to learn. Inert facts don't create a vibrant life experience—they just take up space in your brain. However, higher education does open doors that may otherwise be closed. If one of your Core Desires requires a college degree, you must pursue it. Just be sure it is a Core Desire.

People who go into business for themselves quickly find that there are many things to learn. Without a mentor for guidance, they may have to learn the hard way—finding that much isn't fun and some things are downright unpleasant. To run your own business, you may have to learn about accounting, merchandising, marketing, and sales. If you're

> "I never let school interfere with my education."
> —Mark Twain

hiring people, you'll have to learn all the rules and regulations that govern hiring decisions. Then there are public relations, advertising, and public stock offerings. Learning and educating yourself should always be of benefit for you. At a minimum, it should always be interesting. At a maximum, it should change your life.

Make sure the things you're learning are those you not only need but also want to learn about. If you are driven by a true Core Desire, you will be more than willing to invest time, energy, and money.

> *"What's the difference between school and life? In school, you're taught a lesson and then given a test. In life, you're given a test that teaches you a lesson."*
>
> —Robert L. Carter

One day in a park, I watched two dads and their sons fly glider planes. The gliders had a six-foot wingspan and performed incredible maneuvers. I thought it looked like such a wonderful thing that I'd try it, too. I asked the men where I could find a plane like theirs. I bought one that very day—and it was only $19.95!

Imagine my surprise when I opened the box to find two thousand tiny pieces of balsa wood. It was a kit! I wanted a plane ready to fly. It took me six months just to assemble one wing, and it was no fun at all. To others this may have been an enjoyable hobby, but to me it was hard and boring work. I never assembled the rest of the plane because it wasn't a Core Desire. I wanted to fly a plane, not build one.

Because I never took the time, proper direction, or proper action, I ended up with another failure in my life. The tasks of putting the plane together stopped me permanently. I was motivated from an outside source when I made the snap decision.

Have you ever been that excited about something and started with great enthusiasm, only to not follow through? This is what most goals look like—something that you are initially overjoyed about but soon find you've lost your enthusiasm for once you discover the work involved.

The more interesting and enlightening you are, the more people will welcome you into their lives and the more opportunity will abound.

> *"The educated differ from the uneducated as much as the living from the dead."*
>
> —Aristotle

Learning is not limited to going to school or getting a degree. It's surprising that many people stop feeding their minds after a certain point. For some, that point is high school graduation; for others, it's graduating from college. A large university once took a survey of its recent graduates and found that 90 percent hadn't read a single book since they'd left the university.

Once, while traveling in France for our twenty-fifth anniversary, Marci and I met a couple celebrating their fiftieth anniversary. The couple were in their late seventies, retired, and traveled to someplace new in the world each month. They enrolled in courses at their local university to learn more about each country, and then they traveled to see firsthand what they had been studying.

It is important to share your hard-won knowledge with those who want to learn what you know. Once you attain a body of knowledge or understanding in a specific area, you'll be considered selfish if you only use that information for your own benefit. Share your knowledge with others and be free from that limitation.

Ignorance is expensive in all areas of life, so don't put—or keep—yourself in a box of limited thinking. If you feel that you're boxed in, decide now to think outside the box with the help of your mentors. Your Conquering Force can shatter any limitations you have put upon yourself. Whatever you heart desires can set you free.

Just before I was to conduct a segment of a financial planning seminar, the seminar leader, a brilliant man with a Ph.D. in finance, approached me. He asked me for some background information in order to introduce me properly. He knew who I was but didn't know my academic background. He asked, "Where did you go to school?"

I replied, "Monument Valley High School."

Thinking I was joking, he chuckled. "No, I mean where did you go to college?"

> *"To teach is to learn twice."*
>
> —Joseph Joubert

"I didn't go to college," I told him.

He was shocked. He was also worried about his reputation, since the audience was there by his personal invitation. Seeing that he was upset, I suggested that he concentrate on my accomplishments rather than my academic background.

After I completed my presentation, the man approached me and said, "I've been teaching financial principles for twenty years, and I have a doctorate in finance. You only have a high school education and you are making more money than I am. Something is wrong here. Will you tell me what you think it is?" He was interested in learning from me because it was his Core Desire to earn more money.

"You're not using your knowledge and credentials to create income, you're using them to teach. Teaching is an honorable profession," I told him, "but not if you're interested in making a lot of money."

DO WHAT YOU LOVE

The more you learn about things you're interested in, the more fresh and fun ideas you'll have to mull over in your pursuit of your Core Desires. You'll continually be looking for things to help you be a better parent, salesperson, businessperson, doctor, lawyer, accountant, or PR person. You'll enjoy learning constantly, and you'll discover many benefits.

I know a twelve-year-old boy who can tell you the batting averages of all the professional baseball players, yet he can't recite the names of the four types of clouds that move across our skies. Because he thoroughly enjoys baseball—virtually living, eating, and sleeping it—his constant involvement and immersion in the sport have led him to know a lot about it. And since he isn't interested in clouds, he's never made an effort to learn about them. Regardless of how well his teachers have taught him, the concept holds no interest for him.

My own son struggled with his grades in high school. He thought that he must not be very disciplined or smart, even using the term

> "As long as you live, keep learning how to live."   —Seneca

lazy to describe himself. He had a negative self-paradigm regarding learning and discipline, and he gave himself those labels. His grades were the evidence that these labels were accurate. Yet when it came to learning extensive parts for a school play in a short period of time, he excelled.

When the lead in an upcoming school play was suddenly unable to continue, my son was asked to take his part. The other fellow had four months to learn his lines, and my son had just three weeks. Not only did he learn his lines and perfect his role, he excelled at both. This was ample and undeniable evidence that he was both smart and disciplined—and that doing what he loved made it possible. He had to admit that he was smart, and if he wanted to do something badly enough, the discipline was there.

We are all the same way—we lose interest and don't perform at peak levels if we're not thoroughly engaged. The more interactions you have with others, the more learning experiences you will have, and the more successful you will be in all areas of your life. You'll be happier, too. All this will only happen as a result of learning about your Core Desires.

CONTINUOUS LEARNING

Learning, or the lack thereof, has a dramatic impact on all areas of life. By focusing on the things you want to learn about, you can enjoy continuous learning.

Many students either drop out of college or flunk out because they are studying things that they have little or no interest in. Often students buy into the idea that their parents, friends, relatives, or counselors know what's best for them. Maybe they have been told they should become a doctor because their dad was a doctor. Or maybe their mother has said she'd like an attorney in the family.

Most advice from well-meaning people is not necessarily wrong, but it is not applicable, as it doesn't factor in the students' Core Desires.

One individual I know was sent to college by his parents, although he didn't really want to go. He was happy with his life, but he faced a big adjustment when all his friends left for college. His father was a factory worker, his mother stayed at home. His dad ran a small evergreen nursery for side income and decided his son should major in landscape architecture so he could join the business upon graduation.

My friend muddled along, but the more he looked into landscape architecture, the less he liked it. Higher math was involved, and he hated the subject. Botany and entomology were required, and he barely passed. Finally he discovered that his Core Desire was to become a journalist. In his mind, it boiled down to changing majors, dropping out, or risk flunking out.

He dreaded telling his parents about his desire to switch majors, but when he finally did, they surprised him by telling him that Journalism was a fine major. They were really telling him that their Core Desire was for him to get a college education.

Thousands of college students switch their majors several times before finally selecting a field they feel, in their heart, is right for them. Their decisions may look like whims on the surface, but they could be something much deeper—the belated discovery of their own Core Desires. Most students follow desires that may register only a 60 to 90 on their Core Desire Scale—and as long as there are no barriers, they proceed on their merry way. But once they come to a hurdle, like a lack of interest or too much homework, they reassess their situation or quit. The lucky ones find and pursue their Core Desire until graduation. The others—if they stay on—either change majors again and again, continuing to muddle through and barely pass, or complete a degree that is easy to get or not one they expect to get a job with. Wouldn't it be great if everyone could identify their Core Desires before going to college, or at least within the first year? Just think how much time and money would be saved.

The secret to having a happy life, of which learning is an integral part, is to do what you really love and enjoy. This way, you'll achieve a high level of satisfaction in all areas of your life—at the same time. Others have done it, and there's no reason you can't do so as well. Ongoing change makes continuous learning vital and essential, and learning can be very fun and profitable.

> "Learning is not attained by chance. It must be sought for with ardor and attended to with diligence."
>
> —Abigail Adams

Engaging Your Spiritual Being

The spiritual perfection of man consists in his becoming an intelligent being—one who knows all that he is capable of learning. — MAIMONIDES

The spiritual area—the thinking, feeling, motivating, and refining part of you—affects all aspects of your life. Imagine what you could do and become if you were constantly refining your thoughts, feelings, and behaviors.

> *"The whole of science is nothing more than the refinement of everyday thinking."*
> —Albert Einstein

The whole of life is nothing more than the refinement of everyday living. Imagine how smoothly your life could go if, through a simple refining process, you consistently improved, step by step. In my own experience—and that of many others—I've learned that it is possible to achieve steady refinement of thoughts and feelings in individuals and organizations.

You may wonder how you can motivate your organization, children, employees, or spouse to engage in a process of spiritual refinement. But you have to realize that you can't motivate anyone for more than a moment, because intrinsic motivation flows from Core Desires. True motivation wells up from deep within the recesses of the heart.

Diamonds in the Rough

Our spiritual attributes are often not very refined; they are often like diamonds in the rough—ready to be cut, honed, and polished into gems of great worth. Until they are developed, they aren't esteemed to be worth much. Although your spiritual attributes may only be diamonds in the rough, they are still diamonds—and they are yours—waiting inside for you to be refined and to bring you more joy.

If you wish to experience all the beauty, riches, and happiness that life has to offer, you need to keep the spiritual side of your life strong and continually sharpen your thoughts and feelings. From your thoughts and feelings spring all your Core Desires. Since some desires will motivate and inspire you more than others, you need to focus on your spiritual Core Desires.

When the spiritual area of your life is strong, all other areas of your life will benefit. For example, being open and honest with your spouse helps create and maintain a loving relationship in the family, and that openness and honesty have spiritual roots.

Be More to Do More

Far too many people are trying to *do* more to be happy instead of trying to *be* more. Those who seek more peace and happiness in their lives describe what they "do" in a normal day as feeling overwhelmed and unable to get a handle on their lives. When I write the word *do* on a white board for each activity they perform—from the moment they wake up—within three minutes I have usually written the word *do* almost a hundred times. When I show them that their day is already full of "do-do" activity, they understand it's time to change the daily cycle that steals their peace and happiness. When we discuss why they keep themselves so busy, we often uncover a Core Desire to please others, do well, or feel valuable. As people learn to experience those same Core Desires without doing so much, their lives become a lot less stressful and much more rewarding.

You don't have to perform better or do more to feel loved and successful. Being more—not necessarily doing more—brings the unconditional love and abiding peace you long for. So be open and honest with yourself, be pleasant, kind, and sincere. Be vulnerable, faithful, nonjudgmental, charitable, and thoughtful.

As you refine the positive "be-attitudes" already within you, your life becomes more full of enjoyment and satisfaction. These refined attributes crowd out the negative ones, eliminating the barriers that currently hold you back. You achieve more in life and get there faster. This is possible only when you comprehend the great value of being a person of strong spirituality.

SEVEN STEPS TO POSITIVE POWER

As part of your spiritual refinement, you might seek to eliminate the character flaws that affect your life most negatively and to add as many good traits as possible, since all good traits affect your life positively. Only a clear perception of the exquisite worth of your spiritual traits will cause you to rid yourself of your negative habits and cultivate positive ones. The more negative habits you can weed out, the better your life will become. Some habits may disappear as easily as pressing the delete button on your computer keyboard; others may take years to overcome.

To eliminate the negative and refine your positive traits, follow these seven steps.

1. *Identify your spiritual Core Desires.*

There is great value in discovering your Core Desires within the spiritual area of life—they are crucial to your happiness and joy. Once you know your Core Desires, you will do what it takes to eliminate your inhibiting attributes or habits. Only if the benefits and rewards are worth it to you will you seek the direction and discipline to make the change, pursuing it until you have overcome the pull of your old ways.

Ask yourself, "If I developed that trait, what would it give me that I am not currently getting?" Clearly define exactly what you expect to gain for each trait you wish to add or eliminate. Be aware

> *"Lying is an accomplice to every other form of vice. Deceit, insincerity, cheating are all forms of lying. Lying damages others. Lying subtly permits us to shatter our own self-image and credibility."*
> —Marvin J. Ashton

that not working on a negative trait means that you have decided keeping that trait has a greater benefit to you. If your Core Desire isn't at 100 on your Core Desire Scale, you won't change permanently. If it is, you will persist with enthusiasm and anticipation—even if it takes a lifetime.

For example, suppose your Core Desire is to be highly credible, and to achieve that desire you realize that you must be totally honest. Honesty is one spiritual attribute we would all do well to cultivate. Being deceitful not only costs us our credibility; it costs our society astronomically. Lying is simply not acceptable for you, or to anyone else. When you are completely honest, you never lie, and you just can't lie and be okay with yourself. Lying is a form of self-abuse—it hurts you, and it hurts others. Honesty is a virtue that we should expect from others—and they should expect from us.

Generally there are three reasons we tell lies. First, and more often than not, we lie to protect ourselves or someone else. Secondly, we lie to make ourselves look good. And finally, we lie to gain in money, possessions, ego, or fame. If someone asks you, "What are you feeling?" or "Why are you so quiet?" you may dread telling the truth because—at the core—you are afraid to be honest and don't trust that the truth will be accepted. In fact, you may expect to have a negative experience by telling the truth—and so you tell a lie.

If you want to become a person of total integrity but have difficulty telling the truth, ridding yourself of the habit of being dishonest will move you in quantum leaps toward becoming a better person. Justifying the telling of any untruth for some perceived ben-

> *"Sin has many tools, but a lie is the handle which fits them all."*
> —Oliver Wendell Holmes

efit is unacceptable for the person who values integrity. Don't let anyone tell you that little lies or white lies are not detrimental, because they are. They destroy trust and open the door for bigger lies. In fact, white lies often do more harm than good because others have a hard time trusting people who think that lying in the "right" circumstance is acceptable. Remember that trust is the foundation of all relationships. There are no "white lies." Lies don't come in colors.

When I first went into business, several mentors told me that one of the most important things needed to make money is integrity. "If you don't have integrity, you won't make it in business." Not only is this true in business, it is true in all areas of life. Whatever you do, it must be legal, moral, and ethical. You can then soar to any financial, emotional, or spiritual height you desire. With integrity, you will stand out from the crowd, especially the crowd composed of people who can't be trusted.

> "Each time you are honest and conduct yourself with honesty, a success force will drive you toward greater success. Each time you lie, even with a little white lie, there are strong forces pushing you toward failure."
>
> —Joseph Sugarman

2. *Acknowledge negative traits for what they are. Stop focusing on the problem, and start focusing your faith and energy on finding a solution.*

Being negative or doubting is the same as being faithless. Remember that faith is action out of confidence. If you have little or no faith, you won't take the action needed to get you out of negative situations, conditions, or behaviors. When you are discouraged, financially stressed, or have marital problems, only proper action during those trying times causes you to make the changes needed.

Where can you find the additional faith needed to be more faithful? You may find it in others who have been there and have successfully faced the same problem or a similar circumstance—and prevailed. Borrow from their faith until you have enough of your own.

Remember that a Success Attitude is that frame of mind that allows you to accomplish whatever you want because you *know* you can create the opportunity and make it happen.

> "The faith of the individual in himself, in his fellow men, and in a higher moral order is more important than all the knowledge which the natural sciences have given us."
>
> —Henry C. Link

> "Life teaches us to be less harsh with ourselves and others."
>
> —Goethe

3. *Learn to address and resolve problems.*

With every problem you face, you can leave it as it is, change it, or get out and quit. This applies to marriage, business, friendships, and sports. Many people refuse to take responsibility for their lives and are in denial—or uninformed—about the power within them to choose. They believe that their boss, spouse, fate, or circumstances control their lives. The truth is that we all have far more control over our life's circumstances than we admit. If you can't change negative people, eliminate them from your life. Negative people are like weeds that choke the flowers and fruits from growing.

What we persist in doing becomes easier because our ability to do increases. How fast you find the solution to your problems is in direct proportion to how much you seek a resolution. If it is a Core Desire, you will persist until you find one.

4. *Keep an open mind.*

Be nonjudgmental, because judging incorrectly can hurt your future. Reserve your judgment about people until you know all the facts. How we judge others is how we ourselves will be judged. Do you want to be judged kindly, after all your circumstances are understood? Judging or criticizing is a two-way street—when you don't judge harshly, you'll find people not judging you harshly.

When we pass judgment on others, we assume we are better than they are and believe we know the intent of their hearts. No one is any better than anyone else, and we can't ever know what is going on in someone else's heart.

➡ When I managed the karate studio, I had an instructor who walked a prospective student and his father through the facility, explaining how great karate lessons would be for the thirteen-year-old. The father was convinced and asked the instructor what option would be best for his son. There was a one-year contract teaching basic skills, a two-year contract, or a three-year contract—each designed to help the student reach a higher belt level and proficiency.

➡ The instructor noticed that the man and his son were wearing worn-out Levis and old shirts and made a judgment about the man's ability to pay for the more expensive three-year contract. Rather than risk losing the sale, he recommended the one-year contract. The man agreed and wrote a check. When the instructor saw the name on the check, he immediately realized his error. The father was a wealthy and well-known man who could easily have afforded the more expensive plan. In fact, he could have bought the whole studio.

➡ In the 1950s, Kay Starr wanted to sing with a big band. She went to many auditions where unscrupulous men would try to pick up female singers by promising them contracts. After an audition, one man in particular kept trying to talk to her. At first she ignored him, but finally she told him to leave her alone. The man walked away. Immediately several other singers came up to her and excitedly asked her, "What did Glenn Miller want with you?"

➡ A young man with a lot of talent went to an audition for the Grand Ole Opry. But because of his unusual style, the talent scouts turned him down and told him he would never make it as a singer. Elvis Presley went back to Memphis with a broken heart.

➡ In the early 1960s, an American recording studio needed some hits, so they auditioned an act from England. Making a snap decision based on how the boys looked, the executives turned them down. The Beatles returned to England without a contract.

➡ I remember being on a plane when a man was trying to get his suitcase into the overhead storage space above me. He reeked of alcohol. The flight attendant tried to help him and offered to check the bag, but the man became very angry. Cursing loudly he told her to leave him alone. I judged him to be a loser and mumbled something under my breath. Cursing, he told me to mind my own business and then told me where to go. I was ready for an argument, but then he said, "I just found out that my two daughters had a car accident. One of them is dead, and the other is in intensive care, so leave me alone!" I felt ashamed of myself.

➡ Two young children always went to school in dirty, worn-out clothes, sometimes smelling from not taking baths. At lunchtime these two children would frequently wait until everyone was out of the lunchroom and then rummage through the trash, searching for leftovers. They tried to hide what they were doing, but several of the older boys found them, and ridiculed them.

But some other children, realizing the circumstances of their two classmates, offered to share lunches and snacks, and even conducted a drive to collect new clothes for them.

You will be the reason other people feel good about themselves if you make a conscious effort to acknowledge the good in them—the things they frequently don't see in themselves. Make it part of your life's mission to bring sunshine and light to everyone with whom you come in contact. It's a wonderful way to live, and it creates love and success in our own life.

5. *Remember that growth is a patience-testing, step-by-step, lifetime process, and adversity is part of it.*

When children are learning to walk, first they teeter and fall and try again. Each attempt moves the child a little closer to the Core Desire. The more effort you expend to correct a shortcoming, the faster you'll dispatch it. If it is a Core Desire, you'll find you can change your characteristics or acquire new ones quickly. It may take considerable time and practice for these new characteristics to become second nature to you, but if it is a 100 on the Core Desire Scale, you will pursue it to the best of your ability and eventually refine it to perfection.

Changing the way you react to adversity is also a worthwhile endeavor. This is especially true if you've been—by your own admission and by the observation of your family, friends, or business associates—reacting unrealistically or badly. If you freeze when adversity strikes because you don't know what to do, find a mentor who can give you direction and tell you the proper action to take. Indecision is deadly to both your emotional and your spiritual well-being. Taking proper action is the best way to stop worrying about adversity.

Does this mean you won't get discouraged, afraid, have your feelings hurt, or even get angry because of some of the curves life throws at you? Of course not. You'll experience all of these and more. Be faithful, and take action to help you through the trials.

You must understand and accept that problems, barriers, and even major disasters are a part of life. It is up to you to decide to deal with them, just as you would do if you were to break your arm. If you learn to roll with the punches and ask for help, your adversities will be easier to overcome.

> "We ask for strength; God gives us difficulties to make us strong.
> We pray for wisdom; God sends us problems; the solution of which develops wisdom.
> We plead for prosperity; God gives us a brain and brawn to work.
> We ask for courage; God gives us dangers to overcome.
> We beg for favors; God gives us opportunities."
> —Anonymous

Some adversities may take longer to recover from than others. But good almost always comes from adversity. If you have trouble accepting this, seek others who have dealt with similar hardships, and find out how they coped. In every adversity, there is the seed of an equal or greater benefit.

Whenever you're called upon to handle adversities, realize that you're not alone. People throughout the ages have faced many things with God's help.

There is adversity that you choose, and there is adversity that chooses you. With the adversities you choose, you either don't mind them or you prepare as needed so you can handle them as well as possible. You may choose to start a strict diet so that you can lose weight, increase your mobility, and enjoy more physical activities with your children. Or you may decide to get into shape so you can run a ten-mile race to raise money for breast cancer, even though running ten miles can be hard and painful.

The situation changes dramatically when adversity chooses you. Because you are no longer in control, and there are no expected benefits, you can't see where and when the hardship will end or what the benefits are.

When we choose adversity, the hardship is acceptable because we know what is required, as well as the rewards. However, when adversity chooses us, we complain, worry, fear, and even get angry, because we cannot readily see what we stand to gain.

The antidote for both types of adversity is trust. If you trust in yourself you can endure any situation and take proper action to achieve the best outcome possible. Taking proper action in conditions of adversity involves identifying the problem, recognizing its impact, considering solutions, focusing your resources, implementing the solution, assessing how well the solution is working, and making any necessary course corrections. When you start taking proper action, you start feeling better. Knowing that every cloud has a silver lining may not make you happy when you are in the middle of a raging storm, but the benefits of the hard times that choose you are very real. Sometimes only hindsight can give you this perspective.

We all have an incredible capacity to endure tough times. You must realize that many people have dealt with similar situations and not only survived but also come away from misfortune much stronger and wiser. Trust that this will happen to you, too.

Some of the most marvelous discoveries and scientific advances were made by accident or mistake. The use of penicillin to treat infections is just one example. If those people had concentrated on the problem rather than on the solution, they would never have made the breakthrough discovery.

Some of the most amazing stories only surface after people have faced enormous odds. Lorenzo, a five-year-old boy, contracted a rare, deadly disease, adrenoleukody-strophy (ALD). His parents were told that Lorenzo had just two years to live, but driven by a desire to save their son, they researched the disease and succeeded in finding an effective treatment. Their story was made into a movie, *Lorenzo's Oil*.

There is only one time when an adversity is absolutely devoid of any benefit or gift: the moment when you refuse to see the benefit. Accept the gifts that adversity brings you, and you will be richly rewarded.

6. *Call upon a higher power.*

Everywhere I go in the world, most people tell me that involving God, or a higher power, in their spiritual life is important to them. Most people have a deep and personal belief in God. Spirituality should not be overlooked as a source of guidance, enlightenment, and help.

There will be times when you cannot find the strength to overcome a problem by yourself, and it seems that nobody else can help you either. There will be times when you can't find the answers, and you turn to God. Though you may not understand the methods and purposes of God, if you trust God, you will always have a sense of peace and joy. God always stands ready to help you achieve whatever good you want in this life.

7. *Learn and obey the spiritual laws and principles.*

There are irrevocable laws that govern every realm, be it chemistry, math, music, interpersonal relationships, or parenting. As we learn the laws that govern our Core Desires, we may then obtain the blessings and benefits associated with them. Obedience to these laws will always bring the desired results, just as adherence to any proven formula or recipe does.

> "Before you seek riches, seek ye first the kingdom of God; and after you have obtained a hope in Christ, ye shall obtain riches if you seek them. And you will seek them with the intent to do good—to clothe the naked, to feed the hungry and administer relief to the sick and afflicted."
> —Jacob 2: 18–19, The Book of Mormon

> *"There is a law, irrevocably decreed in heaven before the foundations of this world, upon which all blessings are predicated. And when we obtain any blessing, it is by obedience to that law upon which it is predicated."*
>
> —The Doctrine and Covenants 130:20 of the Church of Jesus Christ of Latter-Day Saints

Failure to apply these laws and truths will keep you from obtaining the benefits that are waiting to be enjoyed. For example, if you fail to water your houseplants, they will turn brown and die, or if you water them too much, they will turn yellow, then die. Knowing just the right amount of water to apply will help them thrive. Similarly, you must learn, and then obey, the laws that govern your Core Desires.

Learning eternal truths and obeying eternal laws have greatly enhanced my ability to have a close relationship with my wife, to have open and rewarding relationships with my children, to earn enough money to live the way I want, and to be very happy. And I am still learning—this is what makes life so exciting.

I know people who are very rich and have many fine possessions, and yet are miserable because they have failed to obey the laws that govern happiness. Some even turn to drugs, alcohol, or suicide to escape. Money and material possessions will not bring you happiness in life. The richest blessings are within the spiritual arena. However, increasing your spirituality can bring you riches, if you seek riches for the right reasons and are obedient to the laws that govern the creation of wealth.

If attaining higher self-esteem is one of your Core Desires, learn to "Love thy neighbor as thyself." There is a reason why God wants us to love ourselves as well as our neighbors. Loving yourself means doing what's best for you, taking care of yourself in all areas of life. You'll eagerly learn truths that will help you be happier; you'll fill your time with good things that uplift and enhance your life. Learn as many truths as you can so you can enjoy the benefits and blessings they bring. If having more faith is one of your spiritual Core Desires, consider the question, faith in what or in whom? God? Yourself? Others? You've got to want what faith will bring you.

In the Bible, God invites people to pray over their flocks. Some would say, "But I don't have any flocks." I don't have flocks of animals either, but I do have a wife, children, and a business. So I pray over these things as my flock. I ask for help in every aspect of my life, especially my marriage and my family. When you add prayer to your Conquering Force, you have the two most powerful forces in the entire universe working in your behalf.

> "Remember God is always a good God. Pray for guidance with the hope and expectation that the answer will come . . . and ask for divine help to be worthy of your blessings. Use your greatest power, the power of prayer."
> —W. Clement Stone

I've mentioned some possible traits, habits, characteristics, and attributes you may wish to change or improve upon. I've also touched upon others you may wish to add. Make the spiritual side of you a priority. Learn the laws and truths that govern the attainment of your Core Desires, keep refining your thinking, feeling, and motivation, and you will experience life more fully. As we seek refinement, we grow, and in growing we become more. This is an ongoing process that will help us to become all that is in us to become.

> "Prayer begins where human capacity ends."
> —Norman Vincent Peale

Conclusion:
The Growth Imperative

Growth is the only evidence of life.
—JOHN HENRY CARDINAL NEWMAN

To achieve your Core Desires—whether they are earning more money, enjoying more intimacy, or having more joy in your life—you need to grow, become more, learn, and change. How fast you grow is within your control; you can experience great growth if you desire it. But you can't just sense a need to change; you can't "sorta" want to be more or have more. If you are willing to grow, life as you have known it will never be the same.

If you choose to grow, you accept the fact that you are not helpless or unable to create the happiness you want in your life. Neither are you limited in your options. What will limit your growth is the inability to identify accurately your Core Desires and unleash your Conquering Force.

> *"Life is about change, but growth is optional."*
> —Bruce Lee

TWO LAWS OF ABUNDANT LIVING

Be willing to become all that is within you to become. Be willing to change, trust, risk, and create opportunities where none existed before.

1. *Be willing to learn and grow.*

If you are willing to learn and grow, you become more and have more. You will need to learn and grow in order to make the changes you desire in your circumstances.

2. *Be open and honest with yourself and others.*

Have past experiences made you fearful or closed? Do you play games with others? Are you totally honest with yourself? Finding your Core Desires is the place to start. To discover your 100s, you must be honest.

To initiate change, you must first accept that who you are and what you have today are largely consequences of the choices and decisions you have made. Instituting change requires that you make different choices now—and in the future. Acknowledge that you always have choices and that you control the choices you make. To make different decisions, you must change yourself—not just the things you do or say, but also what you have your heart set on.

Lasting, dynamic personal growth takes place within your heart. If you can change your heart, you can change your destiny. You may not experience immediate growth just because you accept a truth in your mind; you must also feel it in your heart. Only a Core Desire can cause you to take action on a truth you have mentally accepted. Saying, "I know I should do that," will not bring about change and growth, but wanting it with all your heart will.

Your mind has the ability to learn and apply what it knows; your heart provides the reason to put the knowledge to work. The best way to change your heart is to replace falsehoods and incorrect paradigms with truths and correct paradigms that you feel strongly about—not just understand. Truths can set you free if you embrace them whole-heartedly. The more truths you learn and embrace, the freer you will become. Many of your obstacles will disappear, and you will overcome all others by using your Conquering Force. We choose if—and how—we grow. Our hearts and our minds are under our control, and we can access and mold them. No one else can do this for us. Our Core Desires and our commitment to truth are the chief sculptors of our lives.

People are like Thoroughbred horses in that they are of great value and capable of great speed. Yet they are often constrained by an invisible rope of their own creation. This invisible rope limits how far and how fast they can run. The rope is our wrong, limiting self-paradigm deep inside—made by poor choices that affect our decisions and activities. Until that rope is cut by a new decision, we are unable to run the race of life unfettered.

SEVEN KEY WORDS

These seven words, when used properly, hold the key to finding answers and solutions to every problem, obstacle, or barrier you will encounter. When you are faced with a problem, look at this list to determine what you need to do or be to solve it.

1. *Change*

To make things different in your life, you have to make one or more changes. Change happens all the time, and there is nothing we can do about it. Few things in life are static or permanent, and the "status quo" is never permanent. There are only two things in life that never change: truth, and the fact that *everything* else changes. Regardless of your background, you can become more.

Even when it is forced on us, change is good. We need constant emotional, spiritual, and intellectual stimulation so we can thrive and grow to become all that is in us to become.

If your life is not what you want it to be, let go of what is holding you back, and add to those things that will help you make it the way you want it to be. If everything in our lives is constantly changing, why do we have such a difficult time? Many people resist making changes because they are in a comfort zone. When they look outside and see all the other joys life has to offer, they say they'd like to have them, but not if it means leaving their comfort zone.

Wouldn't it be wonderful if we accepted change and even planned on it? But change is difficult for many people, primarily because we feel fear, inadequacy, discomfort, worry, or stress. To better view change, we should see it as inevitable. Change should not be feared or resented; it should be seen for what it is—a source of growth.

2. *Choice*

Life gives us the *opportunity* to grow. Whether you grow or not is your choice. You can choose to grow and become a happy, spiritual, and emotional giant or stay small. The choices are always yours, and you always have them.

By cultivating the Success Attitude and asking for help from knowledgeable mentors, you can avoid many of the pitfalls in the sidewalks of life. Should you fall in, you'll climb out with their aid. Your future is not in the hands of fate, your boss, the stars, or your circumstances; it is in your choices—the choices you make to determine your path and your destination.

When you are faced with a situation in which you are not happy or not getting what you want, ask yourself, "What am I doing to cause this?" and "What do I have to change in me, about me, or around me to make it the way I want it to be?" Most things that happen to you are either a direct or an indirect result of choices you make.

3. *Truth*

Only truth properly applied will free you from the bondage that ignorance and limited paradigms create. Are truth and being open and honest the same thing? Even though

---

Autobiography In Five Short Chapters

by Portia Nelson

Chapter 1: I walk down the street. There is a deep hole in the sidewalk. I fall in. I am lost . . . I am helpless. It isn't my fault. It takes me forever to find a way out.

Chapter 2: I walk down the same street. There is a deep hole in the sidewalk. I pretend I don't see it. I fall in again. I can't believe I am in the same place, but it isn't my fault. It still takes a long time to get out.

Chapter 3: I walk down the same street. There is a deep hole in the sidewalk. I see it is still there. I still fall in . . . it's a habit. My eyes are open. I know where I am. It is my fault. I get out immediately.

Chapter 4: I walk down the same street. There is a deep hole in the sidewalk. I walk around it.

Chapter 5: I walk down another street.

> *"The object of the superior man is truth."*
> —Confucius

telling the truth is being honest, few are totally open with *all* the truth. When we conceal our real feelings, we're not being open; we are only telling part of the story and not being totally honest. Truth can be obscure if you are not looking for it, but when you have truth as your operating system, you'll stop giving other people or circumstances the power to control your life. You must own the role you play in your circumstances by acknowledging that the truth will free you to make the necessary changes to get what you want.

4. *Trust*

For a truly fulfilling life, trust is essential. You need to trust your mentors, your instructors, your spouse, your doctor, and your boss. Most importantly, you need to trust your own ability to learn, and trust that choosing to make changes will be beneficial.

Many people don't take action because they don't trust that it will make a difference. They don't trust that other people will care. But trust gives you the confidence to take action, and it is the cornerstone of all relationships. If you don't trust others for fear of being hurt, your growth will be severely limited.

Trust comes from making the decision to trust. Although many people feel that trust has to be earned, my motto is to trust everyone until I have reason not to. If someone breaks my trust, then it is difficult for me to know when to decide they can be trusted again. But when, or if, it ever happens, it still involves another decision to trust.

5. *Ask*

To get what you want you must be willing to ask. It is amazing how many people simply will not—or cannot—ask for what they want or need. Sometimes we feel selfish for asking for what we want or need, or we're embarrassed or afraid it will cause problems. Many times we find it difficult to ask for help of any kind, including candid feedback, because of pride or ego. For too many people, asking for direction implies they have either lost their way or are unaware of

what to do. Asking for solutions to our problems means admitting we have problems in
the first place.

But we should all learn that asking for help
and direction is not a sign of weakness; it is the
quickest way to get what you want—from your
spouse, your friends, and God.

> *"Only in growth, reform, and change, paradoxically enough, is true security found."*
> —Anne Morrow Lindberg

6. *Decide*

If you want things to be different in your life, you must decide
to make changes. Action is the direct result of making a decision.
Sometimes we are afraid to make decisions because we aren't sure
of the outcome, but deciding to postpone—or refusing to make—a
decision is still a decision. To make good decisions, you must gather
information from reliable sources and then decide which of the
choices will best suit you and your situation. Some decisions turn
out to be wrong, and others don't give you the results you were
counting on. Therefore, some decisions need to be revisited, and
you must make course corrections.

With the help of mentors, you can decide to choose which way is
best for you to achieve your Core Desires. Once you settle on a plan
of action, there may still be doubts and obstacles in your way, but to
keep from wavering back and forth, simply choose to go for it. If it is
a Core Desire, you will make the necessary decisions until you overcome all hurdles.

7. *Risk*

Our fear of taking risks nips many good ideas in the bud and kills
many hopes and dreams. But we have to recognize that to venture
out on any new path involves taking a risk. Don't let your fear of risk
debilitate you. People who risk little, grow little. If you truly have a
Core Desire, you will face the risk at all costs—and you will learn
and grow.

SELF-ASSESSMENT

Key Word	Always	Sometimes	Never
Change *Can you identify changes you need to make?*	_____	_____	_____
Are you proactive in making changes in your life?	_____	_____	_____
Choice *Do you believe you always have choices?*	_____	_____	_____
Do you look for choices in all areas of your life?	_____	_____	_____
Truth *Are you truthful with yourself and with others?*	_____	_____	_____
Do you seek truths, embrace them, and apply them?	_____	_____	_____
Trust *Is a lack of trust keeping you from what you want?*	_____	_____	_____
Can you learn to trust others, mentors, God?	_____	_____	_____
Ask *Are you afraid to ask for help or direction?*	_____	_____	_____
Do you know whom and how to ask for help?	_____	_____	_____
Decide *Can you make a decision to move forward?*	_____	_____	_____

Key Word	Always	Sometimes	Never
Do you make decisions with the help of mentors?	___	___	___
Risk *Is the fear of risk holding you back?* *Can you gain faith and courage from mentors?*	___ ___	___ ___	___ ___

When you are struggling with a situation and find yourself stuck and not knowing what to do, where to go, or whom to turn to, make use of these seven words to help you assess where you need to go. In every situation, *you* hold the key to your own happiness. Only you can make things different and better. How fast—or how much—is up to you, but both are controlled by your Core Desires.

To create as much success, joy, and happiness in your life as you want, you must know your Core Desires, unleash your Conquering Force, and know that you can—given time—learn whatever you want to learn, create your own opportunity, and overcome all obstacles. You already hold the key to your success in your Core Desires. No outside tools, tactics, techniques, or methodologies have the power or capability to make you achieve success in any area; only your heart-set can do that. When you understand and follow this principle, you will experience the promised blessings.

Your ability to create success and happiness lies within your heart. Your success will always be a direct result of discovering your Core Desires. When you discover your Core Desires and unleash your Conquering Force, you will be successful in any endeavor. You will be able to create and live a life that is full of joy and satisfaction.

Indeed, the truth shall make you free.

Acknowledgments

This book owes its existence to the encouragement and support I received from many people; I cite but a few of them by name.

First, I owe an eternal debt of gratitude to my wife, Marci. She truly has been my inspiration and greatest supporter. Thanks to my children for living lives of honor and integrity—and for loving truth. They are living proof that what I teach works.

I am grateful for my literary agent, Bob Silverstein, whose belief in my concepts and me was both instant and unshakable. I truly appreciate my enthusiastic publisher, Judith Regan, for having the vision of what my message could mean to everyone, and also Liz Lauricella, of ReganBooks, for her masterful skills.

Thanks to Ed Bauer for editorial assistance, ideas, and insights provided to me while writing my book. I am also grateful to Ken Shelton for his help and for the additions of several examples from the pages of *Personal Excellence* magazine.

I shall be forever grateful to those people who were mentors to me regarding my family, business, and in my spirituality. They helped alter the direction of my life significantly.

And thank you to the many thousands of people around the world that have attended my seminars and not only embraced what I teach, but have proven my concepts are the truth by the results they achieve.

About the Author

Jack M. Zufelt has achieved worldwide recognition for teaching people the true cause of all achievement. Through seminars, platform presentations, and audio programs he brings his life-changing message to the world. He has been called the "Wizard of Awes" because of what he says about success and for the way he interacts with his audience.

His life's mission is to impart the truth about—and dispel the myths surrounding—success and achievement to people and organizations throughout the world. Since first discovering the concepts of the *DNA of Success*, he has been helping people achieve better results and create fuller lives with more happiness, joy, and satisfaction.

President George Bush awarded Mr. Zufelt the Presidential Medal of Merit. He has also been honored by the U.S. Senate for teaching Americans how to achieve more in their personal lives and careers.

As a highly acclaimed and honored speaker, Jack has spoken in many regions including the United States, Hong Kong, Taiwan, Australia, Canada, Malaysia, Nova Scotia, Singapore, and the Grand Cayman and Virgin Islands. *Motivation International* magazine selected Jack as one of the top international professional speakers of the decade. *Winners Digest,* a publication for Fortune 500 executives, selected him as one of the most effective speakers in the nation. He is ranked among the "Who's Who" of human potential superstars. His bestselling audio program has been sold in over forty-two countries.

He lives with his wife in Littleton, Colorado.

Jack Zufelt provides the following programs and products for a wide range of businesses, associations, nonprofit and educational organizations, as well as to individuals:

Keynote Addresses
Personal Mentoring
Three- and Five-Day Retreats
Half- and Full-Day Corporate Success Training
Monthly E-zine, "The Z Report"
Business Consulting
FREE Success Reports

Jack Zufelt can be reached at his website: *www.dnaofsuccess.com.*

FREE
ONE-YEAR SUBSCRIPTION

Send in your information below and you will receive a FREE, one-year subscription to Jack Zufelt's popular monthly e-mail newsletter.

OR

Claim your free subscription at this special page at my website:

www.dnaofsuccess.com/freegift

This is a $97 value and I want to give it to you for free!

Please provide the following information:

Name _____

Address _____

City _____ State _____ Zip _____

E-mail _____
             Required

Send it to:

Jack M. Zufelt • 3228 East Phillips Drive • Littleton, CO • 80122

HARPERCOLLINS PUBLISHERS IS NOT THE SPONSOR OF THIS OFFER AND IS NOT RESPONSIBLE FOR FULFILLMENT